Writing and Selling Articles

Joyce White

Quality of Course Inc

© 2000 QC Quality of Course Inc
38 McArthur Ave
Ottawa ON
K1L 6R2

CANADIAN CATALOGUING IN PUBLICATION DATA

White, Joyce.
Writing and Selling Articles

Includes index.

ISBN 1-895492-10-6

1.Journalism—Authorship.2. Authorship—

Marketing. I.Title.

PN4775.W44 1994 808'.02 C94-900211-9

CONTENTS

CHAPTER ONE

INTRODUCTION

I still remember the first thing I ever wrote. I was seven years old and the piece was in bold, beautiful second grade print but it carried a profound message. The tadpole couldn't swim and it drowned.

My teacher was terribly impressed and I was hooked. I just knew I was going to grow up to be a writer.

Grow up is the key. You have to have a certain amount of life experience before you are able to put together something that will sell. The In Group calls it "paying your dues". But there's really only one rule—to be a writer you must write.

My first submission was a masterpiece. It was about the time Stephen King broke into the markets and spook books were hot. I wrote a cross between Lovecraft and King, settled back and waited for a huge cheque, and fame...in that order.

The rejection letter was polite, probably because my inexperience was glaring. I was certain the editor was wrong—he didn't know talent when he saw it. After all, if he could write he wouldn't be an editor!

I proceeded to do all the wrong things. I hired, for a vast sum of money, an "agent" who charged a reading fee so large he had to be good. He said much the same thing as the editor and tried to sell me his book on how to write a book.

About three years later, with no sales under my belt and boxes full of rejected manuscripts, I decided I'd better approach this from a different angle. It was obvious that the obsession to write wasn't going to go away so I'd better find out how to do it properly.

I started to listen to what people told me. I took writing courses. I joined reading/writers' groups. And I lowered my sights.

I wrote a 750 word article about something I knew, targeted the right market, and sold it for $75.00. There will never be another feeling like the one that validated my existence as a writer! My second article sold for $150.00 and I was sure I would never again see a rejection letter.

Not so. I saw a great many but, the problem was, I didn't know how to read them. Editors, trying to be helpful, would say...flesh it out or show, don't tell. Good pieces of advice that meant nothing to me. Throughout this book, you will learn what it is you are being told.

In the beginning I was shy about using my own name. As soon as I started to write, I envisioned the people who would know what I thought. This was a great inhibitor.

I acquired, for forty dollars, a dba (doing business as) and set out to give my talent to the world. My inhibitions scattered and I became proud of what I did, especially if it was published. I told everyone I knew that this was me.

I still have the dba. I never use it unless I'm telling a story where I don't want the people involved to be identified through a connection with me.

The first year I sold 3 articles. The second year, 14. Why these sold when others did not was simple...I knew my subjects and I knew my markets. Hopefully, by the time you finish reading this book, you will too.

It does come down to paying your dues. The same phenomenon that says, "come back when you have experience," applies here. You must somehow amass credits without having tear sheets (published samples of your work) to give credibility to your submissions.

It's not easy to get an editor to take a chance on an unpublished writer so sometimes you have to give your work away for copies or for 1/4 cent a word.

I remember wanting to get into a certain USA publication and selling a 1500 word article, with 6 photographs I never got back, for $25.00. I'm still selling to this market but I now invoice with my submissions...and I get all my photography back.

How this happened is simple. I met my deadline. I sent clean copy. I was pleasant and co-operative, even when they asked for a rewrite. I didn't say, "For $25.00?!"

I submitted to them again, right after acceptance, with a piece I knew they wanted. They came back with another $25.00 offer. I refused and asked them to send the manuscript back. It was Easter Sunday when the editor phoned and asked me how much I wanted.

The more professional you are, the more money you make. But don't give up your day job for a very long time.

If you are a writer you have to write. You cannot learn the dedication, the ability to cope with YoYo emotions—frustration/elation/rejection/success. The only thing you can learn is the mechanics.

I hope you are a writer because, if you are, you have an exciting time ahead of you.

CHAPTER TWO

GETTING STARTED

The image you portray is most important. Remember, you are asking someone miles away to hire you sight unseen.

The letter, bearing letterhead, that arrives on an editor's desk is apt to be read more seriously than the letter typed on copy paper, no matter how well done it is.

The expenditure need not be prohibitive. Design what you want on the computer, print it out, and trot it down to your local copyprint shop. Choose the best paper you can afford and you're all set for a fraction of the cost of professionally printed letterhead. If you don't have a computer, someone you know has. Return the favour, someday.

Business cards are an unnecessary item—I thought. I changed my mind when I was in the company of a group of freelance writers and editors who were busily exchanging their cards and scribbling little notes on the back.

I had a choice. I could pass out bits of paper torn from a notebook or I could make myself scarce. I made myself scarce and lost the contacts.

These cards are an asset when sending queries, requesting information on submissions or source material, introducing yourself to anyone in the writing community. Keep them simple, say only what needs to be said, and keep the price down.

For years I worked on a typewriter, first very manual, then electric and then electronic. I fought against the purchase of a computer. I was not user friendly!

My colleagues told me about the advantages: increased output, being able to work on more than one thing at a time, spell-checks and dictionaries and lower costs. My editors said things like, "what disk can you supply?"

I still didn't want anything to do with a computer. I could be an eccentric, inefficient writer if I wanted to be. Then I wore out my second electronic typewriter and my days were numbered.

It took exactly three weeks to learn to use this thing competently. I didn't need weeks of special courses and it doesn't destroy manuscripts with the flick of a wrong button. It does everything everyone said it would and it feels wonderful to tell an editor I can supply the disk.

If you're still computer shopping, buy only what you need, in the programme you are most comfortable with, but be sure you can upgrade if you have to. Stay with the companies that service what they sell. Discount isn't!

Setting up an office deserves all of your attention. You are going to spend a good part of your life in there—alone—so you'd better like it.

Think about the colours that make you feel relaxed and happy. Try and put everything you need into that one room so you're not running from place to place for books, paper, phones, and so on.

I have taken the smaller, front bedroom and converted it...sort of. It's bright, with a large window, and that's important to me. You may prefer not to have the distraction of a window but I do a lot of my thinking staring into space so I want a space to stare into.

There are three usable walls that allow placement of a lot of furniture and equipment. It houses a large pine desk (voice phone, adding machine, books) and chair, a typewriter table and typewriter (for envelopes and labels), a two drawer filing cabinet, a second-hand store teak table (holds the computer and fax phone and also supplies a large work space if the leaves are up), the matching buffet (printer on top and paper, stationery, etc. inside) a small bookcase, cot with lots of pillows to curl up on when reading manuscripts, etc, and a TV that often burbles in the background.

There is not much floor space left to vacuum and I like that. It's efficient, well-lit and ventilated, and I have everything at my fingertips.

The non-usable wall is a large closet that contains files boxes, copies of manuscripts and boxes of paper.

Your filing system is something that you will work out over time. Start with a few folders in a card- board box or file box. Later, buy a cabinet. You'll know what you need.

Set up your files in such a way that you have a cross-filing system. I have a card-index with one 3x5" for each manuscript name and word count. The information on this card includes the date and place where the story was sent, the editor's name, and short notes about status (acceptance/date, rejection, phone conversations).

I cross reference with a card set up in the publication's name. This information includes the manuscript name and date sent, any comments made when rejected/accepted or status if still out.

An OUT card holds only the names and dates of manuscripts out, crossed off when they are returned or accepted. I find this invaluable for easy reference. It tells me it's time to write or phone the editor and see what is happening with the submission, or that payment is overdue, or what's being published this month.

The last reference card is a record of monies in, the dates and the amount. This saves me from digging through the accounts files if I want to verify something. It's also useful when the writing life starts to get to me. Nothing like a quick adding up of income to either lift you out of the doldrums—or add to the depression!

All correspondence is in the filing cabinet under the publication's name, along with their guidelines and copies of the magazines that hold my work. Tear sheets (photocopies) of published articles are kept separately so they are easily accessed when I want to include samples with queries or submissions.

Reference material, ideas files, extra copies of magazines, materials not often in use, are in file boxes. My system evolved with my career. So will yours.

It's very important to keep a record of all phone calls and conversations, not only for tax purposes (dealt with in a later chapter) but because you're going to forget something the minute you hang up the phone.

I keep a lined pad and pencils on top of the desk by the phone. Also, I can record on my phone so it makes keeping track of details easier.

I have this "flip into cool" mode the minute an editor is on the line. It sounds very professional but it displaces my memory! Notes are a must. There is nothing worse than calling back to find out what they said.

Build a good reference library. Start with those books you know you're going to use all the time. For example, THE WRITERS' MARKET, a good dictionary, a limited amount of good "how to" books, almanacs, encyclopedia and facts books.

Joining a writer's book club and subscribing to writer's publications such as WRITER'S DIGEST, requesting books for Christmas and birthdays can speed this up.

Unless money is no object, don't buy books you're not familiar with. I check them out at the library first, see how much I use them, and then make a decision.

Because office space is limited, I keep only those books which I'm using at the time. The rest are in bookcases in the family room and a rotation system works well.

Everything's in place. You are a writer. Maybe unpublished, but nonetheless a writer. Say it with pride.

Now you must write. Don't wait for the spirit to move you—it won't. Creativity breeds creativity. Don't get discouraged. Just keep writing. Every day.

Editors are always looking for fresh, new talent. Somewhere out there is the one person they have been waiting for. It could be you.

Publishers are in the business to make money so you can sell a well-written piece even if you are completely unknown. They don't care who you are—they care that your piece is something people will want to read.

And, when life's darkest moment strikes, sit back, put your feet up and think of all the now famous writers who couldn't sell their work!

CHAPTER THREE

THE WRITING LIFE

You have chosen a solitary life, a sure cure for "who am I?" It's a rewarding life; a life that builds character and strength; that allows you to live out your dreams.

You wait each day for the mail because it always holds something that will surprise you. The article you were sure missed the mark was accepted, the one you knew was perfect, rejected. There are press releases and market material and requests for work. And, once in a while, there's a letter from someone who read your work.

You see your name in print above your thoughts and observations, a thrill that never decreases. You meet exciting people with interests paralleling your own, and interview people who never fail to teach you something.

You learn what it's like to be exhausted when a deadline is looming and your muse took the day off. You get to know that little churning in the pit of your stomach that says you've written something really good.

I've spoken about image and now I would like to take that one step further—professional ethics. There is the obvious. Never plagiarise a work. Not only is it unethical, it's illegal. But what about the things that aren't so obvious? Editors, for example.

Don't lose sight of the fact that they are human. When they've done a good job, tell them. Always take the time to write to an editor who has commented on your work.

The rejection letter that offers advice is the next best thing to getting accepted. It means your submission has been read carefully and someone saw enough promise to take time out from their busy schedule to help you. It means, try this market again. Soon.

The editor's work load is horrendous. Do as much as you can to help him make a decision in your favour. Let him know you're familiar with the publication, that you will meet your deadline and stay within the word count. Tell him you are willing to make revisions, if necessary.

And if you have to rewrite, do it pleasantly.

Displaying artistic temperament to anyone except your dog, your cat, or your significant other will get you nowhere.

The editor, in turn, will remember you as being co-operative. You might be rejected but when you send another query, it will be considered. Also, if an editor is seeking a writer for an assigned piece, you could be called.

One of my first assignments came over the phone. I thought I understood what was expected but when I submitted the finished piece, I was way off the mark.

The editor was pleasant when she called with the news that they didn't pay a kill fee (partial payment for assigned work completed but not accepted). I took a deep breath and asked her to let me try again.

This time, I conducted the interviews I should have done in the first place. I waited to get photographs from the people involved. There were long distance phone calls to Hawaii and Los Angeles whose cost I absorbed.

The piece was good and it was accepted, but I made about 35 cents. Had I negotiated it properly and submitted to the editor's guidelines, I would have covered my expenses and I would have written it once.

The point is, I didn't let the market go. The editor remembered me and the next time I sent her a query she knew my work. Over the years, I've sold many articles to her and I've only written them once.

It's most important to know the editor's name, spelled correctly. Market information publications can be out of date so if you don't know for sure, double check.

Get a current copy of the magazine and read the masthead (the page that lists editors, contributors, addresses). Not only will it give you the name, it will give you the departmental editor to whom your query should be directed.

This is important. When I began to send out queries and manuscripts, I always addressed them to the top: the editor-in-chief (wrong) or the publisher (very wrong). This is a sure-fire way to get your work lost in the system.

A publisher who receives a manuscript drops it on an editor's desk; an editor unknown to you. He might read it but it's unlikely because when he finally gets through the slush pile (unsolicited material), he sees something that's not addressed to him.

Time drags on. You wait and wait to hear when the periodical is going to publish your masterpiece. Nothing. Finally, you write or phone and no one has ever heard of you or your submission. If you're lucky, they'll invite you to re-submit, maybe tell you where to direct the material. It's far better to do it right the first time.

If there has been an editorial change, pencil it in your card-file and also the market source you are using. These changes will show up in return correspondence, market newsletters and publications such as WRITER'S DIGEST. Scan your local newsstand for the latest market information periodicals that target your area of interest.

The dos and don'ts of simultaneous submissions will be endlessly debated. Most professionals agree that it is unwise to submit to more than one editor at a time. I know it seems forever before you hear about your manuscript but you can save yourself a lot of grief if you play by the rules.

I listened to both schools of thought, those that said, "Time is money—send it out. At worst you will get into a bidding war", and the side that said, "It's not fair to an editor to spend all that time reading only to have you tell him you've sold elsewhere."

My instinct said the second opinion was right and I stuck to it for years. Then I weakened and decided to take a chance. I sent a query to competing markets, telling myself it was unlikely both would accept.

One came back with an offer I felt was too low. I thought I was turning it off when I said I couldn't do it for less than…, quoting a generous figure instead of simply withdrawing it.

In the meantime, the second market showed interest. I sent the full proposal. Then the first market met my terms plus a little more. So did the second market.

I knew I had to play it straight or I'd tarnish the image I'd so carefully nurtured. The worst thing I could have done would be to let both of them purchase an article neither knew the other had. I accepted the first offer and sent the editor the completed piece, with photographs.

I wrote the second periodical and told them exactly what had happened…and apologized all over the place. I wrote a different article on the same subject, assuring them it was different, and sent it off with photography. It was rejected with a form letter, and it took an editorial change before I was able to sell anything to that publication.

It is possible to resell and how this is done will be discussed later in the book. Multiple submission is not the way to do it.

There are publications that state they will consider simultaneous submissions providing they are told this is what you are doing. I'm convinced the amount of effort an editor puts into reading is less if he knows there are others doing the same thing.

I've had the most success with: "While I am not making simultaneous queries (or submissions) I am actively seeking a market and would appreciate a prompt reply." If I do not hear in a reasonable length of time (3-6 weeks, depending on the publication) I follow it up with a phone call.

That is about the only time you do phone an editor. Never call a publication and pitch (tell your ideas) over the phone. The person at the other end of the line is busy and the impulse to say no is usually the one they follow. A query letter gives the editor time to consider your story. If it's a good one, you'll hear.

The editor likes your idea. You've received the phone call that says—go ahead. Be smart. Establish the ground rules right from the beginning. Find out how much you are going to be paid—and when. Ask what expenses are covered. Long distance phone calls and couriers can really add up.

Establish if they will accept phone calls or faxes should questions arise. Make sure you know when your deadline is—many publications are working 3-12 months in advance of the print date so if they say it's for a November issue and this is only June, it doesn't necessarily mean you have a whole lot of time.

Know your maximum and minimum word count and stay within those limits. Request a follow-up letter to confirm your assignment, including all contractual details. Then, make sure you do what you said you would.

Editors move. (I've worked with one editor on 3 separate publications.) They talk to other editors.

Above all, they like to build a stable of reliable writers that can be called upon to produce, quickly and efficiently, assigned material.

The writing life demands that you learn to accept rejection letters with grace. You must also understand the hidden messages in the different types of letters.

If you are getting nothing but form letters, submission after submission, you'd better sit down and re-think your work.

Form letters are the norm when you're starting out. There seems to be some little gremlin that sneaks into your work and flashes...New Writer...New Writer.

There are some traps that beginning writers do fall into and these will be discussed later.

A step up from the form letter is the one that has a few scribbles on the bottom directed to you. It might say something along the lines of: liked this but not for us, or we're full—try in 6 months, or the editor might give you some writing tips. Listen to them.

Many editors are using the rejection letter with multiple choice reasons. They tick the ones that apply. While this is not a dialogue, it is better than nothing. At least you know why you were rejected.

If you are lucky enough to get a rejection LETTER, celebrate...and thank the editor for taking time to comment on your work. You'll know you've come to terms with rejection the day you exclaim, "I just got the best rejection letter!"

When you live the writing life, you will find it creeping into every part of your being. No matter what you are doing, some idea, some line for a story, some lead for the next article, will be invading your thoughts.

You will notice things about people you never did before. Carry a notebook because you will see a story in every occurrence—in your life and everyone else's. My kids hate me.

The writing life means WRITE. Every day. If you can't think of a topic start with what's around you...your family, your pet, the late milk delivery and what it did to breakfast. Anything. Just write.

Soon you will fall into the habit of writing and a schedule will develop. It will be the one that suits you. Remember to take some time out for exercise and laughter because there is no such thing as Writer's Block. There is Writer's Burn Out!

CHAPTER FOUR

FINDING MARKETS

The next step in the business of writing is finding a market. That's right—before you have written something to sell.

I can almost hear you saying this is backwards. Everyone knows there must be a product before you can market it. One time, I would have agreed with you.

It was exactly the practice of writing something that inspired me or interested me that produced the boxes of rejected manuscripts languishing in the basement. I won't even mention the cost of postage and paper. So, let's look for markets.

Start at the beginning. Go to the library and find periodicals that carry topics which appeal to you. Unless you have a specific reason for wanting magazines at home, don't purchase any. The paper war will get tough enough without adding to it unnecessarily.

Read until you become familiar with the publication. Jot down the editor's name, the address, phone and fax numbers, from the masthead. When you have a manageable list, say ten, write the editors, introduce yourself and request their guidelines.

Keep the letter simple and, of course, written on your letterhead.

03 July 1994
Ms. B. Smith, editor
OUTDOOR HIKER
Grass Publications, Inc.
555 John Avenue
Second City, B.C.
6V8 2M3

Dear Ms. Smith:

I am a writer breaking into the freelance market. I would like to submit to OUTDOOR HIKER. Please send me your guidelines and any immediate market requirements.

Thank you.
Sincerely,

John Jones
encl: SASE

Enclose a SASE (Self Addressed Stamped Envelope) in all your requests and correspondence. Not only does this practice signal the editor that you are a professional, it ensures an answer.

The next step is to build a file of all reliable market information. This includes the guidelines that the editors send you.

In the beginning I had one file folder for all this information because it was an easy way for me to find what I needed. As I began to write query letters and make submissions, and the paper grew, I set up a file under each publication's name. Depending on space, you may want to do this from the start.

Notes in my card file summarize which periodicals are promising and if tear sheets are included in the main files. I read through these files from time to time, keeping myself up to date.

Make it a habit to save copies of all your correspondence. When I reply, I print out the duplicate on the back of the editor's letter, thereby giving me access to dates, reference numbers, requests and replies on one sheet of paper.

My files on publishers, including guidelines and editorial correspondence, are housed, alphabetically, in a two-drawer filing cabinet. The letters in these files are kept according to date.

Reference material (clippings, notes, etc.) and manuscript copies are kept in file boxes on the floor of the closet. They are easily accessible and it saves room. Business files, such as office expense, receipts, accounts owing, are in the file drawer of my desk.

Market material can be found in places you'd never expect. Ever think about junk mail? It's filled with treasures. The magazine that's trying to attract a subscriber gives detailed sampling of their editorial content.

Read this mail carefully. Send for the guidelines of those you find interesting and, when it arrives, staple the promotional material to it. Instant, complete reference.

There is an abundance of source material available. I can't say it too often—don't buy anything until you know you are going to use it.

Study the books you think you can't live without in the library, in book stores, or borrow a friend's. You will need WRITER'S MARKET, a United States publication that carries some international markets, and its a good idea to have THE CANADIAN WRITER'S MARKET. If you are submitting to Great Britain, Australia, or other overseas markets, have the book store order the appropriate material.

I purchase market books every two or three years. In the meantime, I pencil in changes. I rely on support material—trade papers, writer's magazines, bulletin boards, writer's meetings, and correspondence to keep me up to date

Clearing House offers allow you to purchase a subscription at discount prices. You may find this an easy way to familiarize yourself with several issues of a particular publication. As one subscription lapses, replace it with another that has market potential.

Read everything and have "clip and save" files. These are part of the reference files I keep in boxes. They are set up under subject, ie: cats, dogs, travel, women's issues, health, environment...anything that I might want to write about someday.

Local newspapers are often a market for beginning writers. While the features are staff written, the opinion pages usually welcome freelance pieces. The pay is low so established writers show little interest.

Contact the appropriate editor and see if he is interested in your submission.

Don't discount television as source material. Ads, promotional material, special offers, will often supply you with market ideas.

Association with other writers can be a market source. I have had many tips from friends, as well as introductions to editors. Periodical writers groups also keep you up to date, through word of mouth and newsletters, with who's buying what.

Special attention should be given to markets outside your area. Canadian and United States Markets are comparable. Return postage is the only problem. This is easily overcome by the use of International Coupons, purchased at the post office. One coupon equals one first-class letter stamp. However, the cost is considerably higher. If you have $5.00 return postage, this can be cumbersome.

I have a friend send me stamps from the United States which I then place on SASE to USA publishers. Also, a US Dollar bank account allows me to write a cheque should I wish reply by courier.

Overseas markets are handled in exactly the same way.

Remember that you are trying to get into the magazine, not necessarily be published by it, although that is the ultimate purpose. You want to attract the eye of an editor and make a positive impression so he knows you have something to offer.

To this end, you need to know the magazine's content, the advertisements and the illustrations. All of them tell you something.

The content puts you in touch with the editorial policies of the publication. If you are writing about child care and the magazine is carrying hints on retirement, this is not the market for you.

Have a look at the length of the articles and the authors' names. If they are publishing 4000 word features written by people like, I.M. Wellknown, and you are a novice comfortable with 750 words, save that market for later.

Study the editorial pages because they tell you what is staff written and what is open to freelance. Many periodicals welcome short "department" submissions but will not consider anything for the "regular" features.

Are the titles pretentious? Do they carry a strong political bent? Are they serious, humorous, or aimed at an "age group"? Ask yourself, does my idea fit here?

The advertisements give you a good clue as to editorial policy because they are trying to sell to the same people you are targeting. Is the focus of your article in conflict with these advertisers? If so, forget submitting there. The publisher will not risk offending those who pay his bills.

Publications without advertisements are markets that you should consider carefully. Often they do not have the funds to support freelance writers and pay in copies only. While this may be an option when building credits, it's not later on in your career.

Illustrations accompanying the articles will tell you what the editor is going to expect from you. If they are heavily illustrated with exceptional photography and you are unable to supply quality material with your submission, it is unlikely the piece will sell to that market.

Many writers work closely with a photographer or have access to stock shots (a photographer's inventory). This is a relationship you might want to build and will be dealt with in more detail in a further chapter.

Doing a market analysis can help you target the publication. Choose the magazine you wish to query. How many pages? How many of these pages consist of advertising? Break down the ads—how big? What subject?

For example, the magazine has 80 pages. 30 are advertising. In most cases, the ads are whole page, full colour. The contents include: fashion clothing, food, alcohol, jewellery, furs, travel, skin care and perfume products.

You know this is a woman's magazine, geared for the upper-income, professional female. If your article is on home schooling—you have the wrong magazine. If it's on exotic resorts in the Caribbean, you have a shot.

Never stop studying the market place. Read every chance you have. Browse book stores and libraries. Keep your eyes open and when the idea hits you, you'll be ready.

CHAPTER FIVE

FINDING IDEAS

If you think your ideas are going to arrive on the wings of inspiration, you're wrong. Writing is 2% inspiration and 98% perspiration!

The trick of keeping a pencil and paper beside your bed to jot down night-time flashes of brilliance is purely fiction. It doesn't happen that way. If you doubt this try it and, next morning, read the genius of your words. Wait for a revelation and you'll starve. Writing is work, just like any other job!

Your best ideas will come from the things you know. Novice writers often overlook the obvious. They try to target markets that are out of their range of experience. While it's not impossible to write about things you haven't lived, providing you have the technical ability, it certainly makes your work more difficult.

A few years ago, I accepted some assignments dealing with financial problems, scams, and safe investment for a retirement focused magazine. I didn't know a thing about the subject but, hey—how hard can the research be? Very hard, that's how hard.

I spent hours on the telephone with agencies and recorded endless amounts of tape in interviews. I fought for every word I wrote. The series of articles were published but they were dry and colourless...a listing of facts.

Shortly afterwards, I did an article on Kona Village, Hawaii, outlining their wedding/honeymoon package. Kona Village is one of my favourite places in the world and the piece was as much of a joy to write as it was to read.

I had such intimate knowledge of the hales, (house) the beach and the people that the words flowed. I have sold this article nine times, reworking the focus, and each time is as good as the first. Later, you'll learn how to do this.

Some of the best ideas come from pets. We all tend to humanize our animals so they carry a personality that shines through the written word.

We were in the Caribbean for a time. A hurricane drove most of the island's rats inside to live with us and I found this intolerable. Enter, one cat.

I had no intention of acquiring a short-term pet but she did the job in a matter of hours and I fell in love. When it was time to return home, leaving her behind was unthinkable. She would travel with us.

The flight was long and I was worried. I bought her a cat-ticket so she could be in the cabin with us. The trouble was, only the First Class section offers cat service. I was convinced she was worth it.

Ticket in place, I visited a once pink and yellow hut where the "vet" lived to ask if there was something I could give her to make the trip less stressful. He presented me with The Little White Pill. It would "be the trick".

I'll say it was! The cat slept all the way to the airport only to surface in a drunk and disorderly state the minute we tried to board the plane.

The airline wouldn't let her in the cabin and they didn't care how much the ticket cost. She went baggage. We went First Class. To make matters worse, we missed the connecting flight home because we had to find her on the carousel. We should have followed the noise!

We learned the plane had gone, that no hotel would take us, that we would have to sleep in the airport unless we wanted to charter a plane, at 2:00 AM.

We chartered the plane and then got customs out of bed to stamp us into the country—with a cat not carrying entry papers. We must have looked as bad as we felt because the custom's officer didn't do all the terrible things to us that he could have.

I carried the cat mumbling—you're going to pay for this! Pay she did.

The article sold as the drunk cat trip, as travelling with a cat, as the safety of medications, as cats in hurricanes, as how to get a cat into a country. Then we had all the other aspects of the story...the Caribbean side. The experience made me more money than the fares, and it still sells.

There is always room for personal experience stories. If you have the ability to laugh at yourself and to put it on paper, you have a ready market. Don't forget your family's experiences. Or your friends.

When my husband had hip replacement surgery, he wasn't home from the hospital before I had the article sold. A statement often heard in our house is: "Don't write this, Mom!"

Ideas will come from the things you read in newspapers. There might be a piece covering a place you have visited. It sparks memories unique to you and you know you can give the story another slant. Cut it out and save it in the "ideas file".

An article might be unfinished, from your point of view. Clip and save for a follow-up story. News items invite comment for the Opinion page.

Your clip and save file should contain things you have collected from magazines, newspapers, publications found in secondhand stores, brochures and flyers. It should contain things that have happened to you, your family, your friends. It should be full of notes about events you've seen and ideas that you've had.

At first, keep these gems in one folder but later, as they become part of the paper war, separate them into topics.

These might be: animals, politics, travel, women's issues, men's issues...whatever interests you.

As they grow, separate and separate, again. Animals becomes: dogs, cats, horses, etc. Dogs may later break down into breed, care of, health problems...you get the idea.

Read every chance you have. Everything you read will trigger something in you—a memory, a strong opinion, a humorous incident. I am not talking about plagiarism here, but the way an article will bring some forgotten experience to the surface.

I never read and write similar material at the same time because I tend to pick up the other writer's style if I do. If I'm writing nonfiction, I read fiction. If I'm writing fiction, I read articles or how-to books.

You may not have this problem, but watch for it. Your aim is to develop your own voice not copy someone else's. The purpose of studying other writers' material is for construction, technical ability and a fresh slant on well-worked themes.

Your opinions, your likes and interests, are a treasure trove of ideas. What about your pet peeves? Your political bent? Do you have a cause you are fighting for? Religious magazines are a good market.

I mentioned junk mail before as a source for markets. It's an equally good source for ideas. I get on everyone's mailing list and I scan every flyer, every ad, every promotional idea.

In the mail comes financial news and health breakthroughs, and travel offers. The information is always detailed and always current.

If everything around you fails to trigger an idea, try brainstorming. Write a word on a piece of paper and start asking yourself questions. For example, you have written: salmon.

What do I know about salmon?

How many kinds of salmon are there?

Where do they live?

What do they need to live?

What do they eat?

Are they endangered?

What are people doing to help them?

What are the rules of conservation?

What about fish farms?

Can I get to a fish farm?

Are there differences between farm fish and wild fish?

How do you catch them? Prepare them?

The list could go on for a very long time. The more you discover through the answers, the more questions will arise.

You have pages of dialogue. Now, break it down into the markets that can apply. There's fish farming for an ecology magazine; recipes for homemaker's magazines; how to catch salmon for sports magazines, to name a few. One session of research should produce data for many sales.

Even if you have a great idea that you're sure you can develop, this is a valuable exercise. Doing these steps will bring more and more information to mind as well as show you where the research is weak.

Your aim is to find something in an article that no other correspondent has been able to find. If you can do this, you have made your mark as a good writer.

But, it's not enough to have an idea. You must test it. Ask yourself the following questions.

Is the idea exciting?

Where does the interest lie? What reader group? Women? Men? Children? What subject group? History, humour? political?

How much has been written about the subject?

How can I vary it?

Is it so topical that by the time I write it, it won't be relevant?

Is it informative?

Does it entertain?

What is my purpose in telling the story?

If the article is humorous—am I funny enough to write it?

Do I have enough expertise to write this medical/reference/education article?

Finally, don't tell me about your garden—help me with mine. This applies to many subjects such as holidays, parenting, and home decorating.

One of the most important rules to remember is that nonfiction is TRUE. You must ask yourself, every time you write something, "Is this the truth or have I taken license?"

There is a nonfiction format called, Creative Nonfiction. (We'll go into this later.) Is this what you are writing or are you reporting on an event or telling about a person's life? They are different markets.

It's not enough to simply know your subject. Your thoughts must be turned into something saleable. Think about your reader and talk to him when you are forming the idea.

Stay with one focus. For example, if you are a furniture restorer you could write volumes on the subject. Keep it to "Restoring Grandmother's Chair", or "How To Find Antiques To Restore", or "Different Finishes For That Favourite Antique". Save everything in your ideas file that doesn't fit the theme. You'll use it later.

The final check list before you start to write should include the question of ethics. Have I been too critical? Is this idea spiteful? Am I being responsible?

Some things to remember in nonfiction writing.

1. A writer never takes a vacation from chasing ideas. If you are not writing, you are thinking about writing. Get on a

plane or take a car trip and it will turn into more articles than you ever imagined.

2. Don't tell your ideas before you write them. If you tell your story to someone else, the creative urge will have been satisfied and, if you do write it, the piece will not be as good as it would have had it been fresh.

3. Don't discard an idea because you don't think it's worthwhile. Put a note in the ideas file. If it's not written up on it's own, it will be used with something else.

4. Don't expect ideas to "arrive" completely formulated and ready to go. An idea is a seed that you must nurture, worry over and develop into something worth reading.

5. Don't preach. There is a balance between objectivity and subjectivity....strive for this. It is possible to put your opinions across without offending anyone.

6. Use a personal slant. Editors can read a brochure just as well as you can. They are looking for unique, professional development articles that draw an original conclusion.

7. Write about the things that interest you even if they have been done before. There are no new ideas—just new approaches. Try a reversal of mood (a serious subject given a slightly humorous bent) or a variation on a familiar topic.

Your idea has passed all the tests. You are certain it's a good one and you're ready to send out that query letter.

It's time to match it with a market. If you've done your research, this is a relatively easy job. Save yourself some time and assume that the query is not going to be accepted by the first or second editor. Make a list, from your first choice down, of all possible placements.

Go through your guidelines and make sure the idea stands up to the requirements. I strongly suggest you don't make simultaneous queries but, if you do, let the editor know.

You are ready to present your idea.

CHAPTER SIX

PRESENTING YOUR IDEAS

You have reached the most optimistic stage in the process of writing and selling articles. You have a wonderful idea. The market has been given careful consideration and targeted correctly. You know your subject inside and out. How can you lose?

Don't assume the editor is going to share your enthusiasm. It's your job to convince him you do have something to offer.

This is where a query letter comes in. It gives you the advantage of outlining your product without tying up your material for months. You will know for sure that you have an idea that's worth writing. If you are able to sell entirely from query letters, before you write the article, you will have a 100% success rate!

Queries are answered in 3-4 weeks, if not sooner. Unsolicited manuscripts can sit for months and are often returned with a form letter that tells you less about your submission than would the reply to a query.

Never forget that you are selling a product and fighting a difficult, buyer's market. Thousands of pieces of mail cross an editor's desk each year so there has to be something about yours that makes it stand out from the rest.

An editor looks for a fresh approach in material geared to his needs. Ideally, he is able to build a stockpile from which to draw as the need arises.

Each month, there are X number of pages to fill. Some are taken up by regular features, some are staff written and some may be written by the editor. How many pages are left over is the chance you have of selling to the publication. Analyze the periodical.

The editor looks through the stockpile, searching for the mix that gives balance to his magazine. If there's nothing suitable, he turns to what's on hand. Yours may be the letter he picks up. Grab his attention.

Five points you need to consider are: catch the editor's attention, arouse his curiosity, tell him why he needs your article, summarize your ideas, urge him on by asking direction.

Lets have a look at each one.

1. CATCHING HIS ATTENTION—The Hook.

There are four main types of openings for every article written. I am using my own material as examples merely because it simplifies permission and rights.

a) ANECDOTE

"We arrived in the Caribbean three weeks before Hurricane David. I recall being asked as we were leaving Canada, "Aren't you afraid of hurricanes?" Hurricanes? What hurricanes? There hasn't been one in 50 years. I should have known they were overdue."

(THE PILL, THE CARIBBEAN, AND THE CAT, I Love Cats, Nov. 1989)

"My husband retired and we became joined at the hip so, when replacement surgery was imminent, I knew I would be involved. He might have the knife, but I was going to be stuck with the stitches."

(AH, MODERN MEDICINE, Today's Times, Sept. 1991)

b) QUOTATION

This can be from a famous person—"To realize Victoria you must take all that the eye admires in Bournemouth, Torquay, the Isle of Wright, the happy valley at Hong Kong, the Doon, Sorrento and Camp's Bay—add reminiscences of the Thousand Islands and arrange the whole around the Bay of Naples with some Himalayas for the background."...Rudyard Kipling

29

(A HONEYMOON IN CAMELOT, Bridal Fair, Dec. 1992)

Or, it can be a quote from an interview. "There is only one thing better than falling in love...and that's staying in love." Nothing more aptly describes the emotion that went into Barbara and Robert Desforges' reaffirmation of their wedding vows.

(A STERLING EVENT, Discovery, Jan. 1989)

c) PREMISE

"Daily, you can pick up the paper and find another story about the current run of get-rich-quick schemes. They promise increased income and tax relief. They promise the good life on some foreign bit of land. They cover three big lies: you will make a lot of money, you will make it quickly, and it's safe!"

(THE LURE OF QUICK PROFIT, Elder Statesman, Nov. 1991)

"There was a time when it was uncommon for Catholics to divorce. If they did, they certainly didn't talk about it openly."

(REMARRIAGE, A SECOND LOOK, Our Family, May 1992)

d) QUESTION

"When I heard of professionally grooming a cat, my first reaction was one of stifled laughter. Who ever heard of such a thing? And why would it be necessary? Everyone knows cats are fastidious."

(PROFESSIONAL GROOMING, Cats, June 1991)

"When does it happen? That day when children look in the mirror and declare themselves keepers of your soul; the day when you are no longer capable of reasonable and rational thinking."

(CHILDREN KNOW BEST, Senior World, Aug 1987)

These are leads to articles but a good query letter often includes the first paragraph as a hook. It not only outlines the focus of the story, but it can capture the editor's attention and make him want to read more.

You may open your letter with one or two sentences that follow these four categories. For example:

a) Anecdote: When I walked into the store, a display of stuffed toys caught my eye. Imagine my surprise when the cat I reached for turned out to be alive!

b) Quotation: "Floral touches contrived by the housewife's hands were very English." Ester B. Arestry said this in her book, The Delectable past. That quotation describes many of today's arrangements....

c) Premise: Children in open learning situations benefit greatly from the experience. I would like to share with your readers what I mean by this.

d) Question: Did you ever wonder how the milk is collected from female salmon? Did you know there is a school in British Columbia that involves the students in the process?

2. AROUSE THE EDITOR'S CURIOSITY

Your letter of inquiry is NOT a chatty letter discussing an idea. You are offering the editor a subject with a unique angle. It is titled, it is real, and you are asking for approval to go ahead and complete the article for publication.

You have opened with a catchy hook. Now, give him a succinct outline. While you do need to convey your knowledge of the subject and the organization of your material, you do not want to overwrite. Simply, tell him what question your article will address. For example:

"I wish to show the reader that many of yesterday's herbal remedies form the basis of today's recognized cures. I plan on doing this by......"

3. CONVINCE THE EDITOR HE WANTS THE ARTICLE

It is most important that you read back issues of the magazine you are querying. Don't bluff—the editor can spot deception a mile away. At best, your rejection letter will suggest you read a few issues of the publication to familiarize yourself with the editorial policy.

Tell the editor why his readers will be interested in your article, what it is about it that makes it different from all the others out there, and why you should be the one to write it.

Example: "I lived with the people for several years and understand the culture. I was privileged to observe many of the ceremonies and found startling similarities between this tribe and our own society. My intimate knowledge of the structure allows me to give your readers an insight they will not obtain elsewhere."

4. SUMMARY

The end of your letter is almost as important as the beginning. In a line or two, summarize what you are doing and why. Example:

"I know this article on the Ganie-Ganie tribe will be important to your readers. Not only does it fit into your editorial guidelines, it also gives a unique perspective on an interesting society. I look forward to writing this for LITTLE KNOWN PEOPLES."

The summary should include a short bio. Outline your writing experience, your education pertaining to writing, credits, and if tear sheets are enclosed. If you do not yet have credits, use: "I am a writer breaking into the freelance market....etc."

5. CLOSING

Urge your editor on by asking him questions. A good way to approach this is to seek direction.

"Would you please let me know the approximate word count, the lead time (your deadline), and the preferred photographic format." (Submission with slide or print).

DO NOT ask about pay schedules at this point. That comes after your query has been accepted.

The best query letter is one page long, HAS NO ERRORS, and has convinced the editor that he needs your article. You have done this by portraying such a positive attitude about your work that you can't imagine the piece could ever be turned down.

Example: Written, of course, on your letterhead.

J.P. Smith, Editor

WOMAN MAGAZINE

555 5th Street West

Anytown, Ont.

Canada M1M 1M1

Dear Ms. Smith:

Did you know there is a new organization offering help to first time mothers? The concept grew when a young mother of four learned the new-born she was fostering was the child of a teenage mom.

This *leading edge article will contain exclusive interviews with the expectant mothers and the companion moms, as well as the founder of the one on one support programme. The stories centring around these mothers' association with each other and the intimacy of the shared birth experience are often humorous and always touching.

In today's society, expectant mothers can find themselves alone with no financial or emotional support. A first pregnancy, an event that should be rewarding, may turn out to be fearful. This article gives hope to those who have no place to turn.

JUST FOR MOMS would fit into your editorial policy because it is an upbeat story about a woman on the move—a woman who is giving something lasting to her community.

I have been writing professionally for 15 years. I am a member of (writer's organizations). A copy of my publishing credits, tear sheets of my work and a SASE are enclosed.

In your reply, would you please state the maximum word count, your lead time, and if you require photographs to be submitted with the manuscript. I look forward to doing this article for WOMAN MAGAZINE.

Sincerely,

A. Writer

*Leading edge is an editorial expression for subjects that have seldom, if at all, been published. They contain goundbreaking material all editors seek.

The article on JUST FOR MOMS sold with the first query. It sold again, after publication with the women's magazine, to newspapers and a local periodical. I also obtained a commitment from the first publication to do updates as the organization progressed.

There are several ways to handle the biographical part of the letter. If you have many credits under your belt, display them but do it with humility.

I enclose separate sheets of paper that list, in sections, my credits in fiction, nonfiction, poetry, books and the writer's organizations to which I belong. It also includes any awards, contests judged, major works pending, and the name of my agent with the observation that she handles only my books.

When repeat work has been done for a publication, I place an asterisk beside the name. This method of organizing my credit sheets lets me add information easily, as required.

In the beginning, I avoided the subject of credits. It's extremely difficult to send a query letter asking someone to buy work when you can't give them a sample of what you can do.

Seek out those markets that don't demand you query first. Research them carefully and send them a completed manuscript. Take whatever is offered you, even if that's payment in copies only.

When you have one credit, you can query with: "My credits include MEN IN SPORTS. The tear sheet is enclosed....etc." You will be surprised how quickly credits will mount up once you've broken into the market.

Occasionally, an editor will come back to you requesting a proposal. Don't panic. A proposal is nothing more than a LONG query.

You can expect to detail those points you've already outlined and, perhaps, add a few more. The proposal should be about five pages long and include more information on expected word count, quotes, and story progression.

While proposals are expected in the book market, they are not common in the magazine/periodical market. An editor should be able to tell from a query exactly what it is you have in mind. The only time a magazine asked me for a proposal was for a piece that involved the serialization of a story.

When the editor answers you, whether it be with acceptance or rejection, write and thank him for his time.

If accepted, confirm your understanding of the assignment. This is important for two reasons. The editor works well in advance of the time the magazine goes to print. Verifying your submission secures your place, making his job easier because it removes all doubt about your agreement.

It also eliminates any chance of misunderstanding. You are confirming deadline, word count, subject, and payment. (The editor should have told you how much he is willing to pay at the time of commission. If he failed to do this—ask!) In future, when you submit a query, the editor will remember your professionalism.

Perhaps the single most important thing to remember about a query letter is that it has to be complete enough to demonstrate that you know your subject as well as the market to which you are submitting.

Frequently, novice writers will fall into traps. Be aware of the following:

1. Make sure your query is addressed to the appropriate editor, name spelled correctly.

2. Be professional in your approach. Don't get "chatty" and don't sound like a "letter to the editor."

3. Be familiar with the magazine even if it means spending hours in the library reading back issues as well as current copies.

4. Concentrate on the subject you are covering and include only enough personal information to give the editor some idea of your level of expertise, education and experience.

5. Keep a balance in your letter. Never criticize the publication but, on the other hand, don't get all "flowery". If you subscribe to the magazine or if you can give a sincere compliment, fine. Editors are human and like to be told when they do a good job but the only incentive for purchase will be the quality of your submission.

6. Always include a working title, a unique angle and a SASE. Make your query as interesting as any cliff-hanger.

7. Don't send simultaneous queries.

8. Don't send query letters for fillers or articles under 1000 words. Submit the completed piece.

9. Write in your best style, with no errors. BE PROFESSIONAL!

If your query has been accepted, follow it up with another one while the editor knows your work. Make this one as good, if not better, than the first. This is how you build a relationship with an editor.

Eventually, someone will phone and say, "I want to include an article on saving stamps. Can you do it for me?" This is the next best thing to staff writing. The Editorial Commission!

One of the hardest parts of being a writer is the waiting. As a general rule, the longer you wait for an answer to a query or a submission, the better it is.

If you are rejected on the first mail after the editor received your letter, maybe you'd better rethink the idea. If you have waited 6 weeks for a reply, it's time to find out what's going on.

The easiest thing to do is phone the editor. Have a copy of your correspondence handy when you tell him what you've submitted, and when. Ask if the query was received. Often, a conversation will take place that gives you insight into the way the editor works, as well as the magazine's requirements. If the editor isn't interested in this piece, he may tell you what he needs for future issues.

One last word on the subject of queries—don't sit back and do nothing while you wait for a reply. You may be writing the article, but you may not. So, get busy. Research more markets and send out more letters.

Just think of the fun you're going to have when they're all accepted and the deadlines are a week apart!

CHAPTER SEVEN

RESEARCHING THE ARTICLE

The query has been accepted and you have an article to write. The preliminary research is completed but all that's told you is that you have access to enough information to do the assignment. Now, detailed facts must be gathered.

Research is fun. You find all sorts of bits of information that don't matter at all...like it takes 5,000 bees all their lives to make one pound of honey. Who cares? You might—for a later article on bees or honey or city farming or interesting insects.

File all the secondary information in research files set up the same way as your ideas files. Divide and divide again as the paper war continues. Later in this chapter we will get into storage and retrieval.

Keep in mind you are writing for profit. You do not want to pay a researcher and you do not want to belong to an expensive computer network.

You want to use the library, the single most useful tool in research. There are computer links that are free except for the modem/telephone charges incurred by you. Check the publication date of all accessed material to make sure the data is current.

Don't overlook the use of university libraries and data banks. Charges, if any, are minimal. Some organizations have libraries containing local history. These, too, can prove invaluable.

Archives and newspaper morgues maintain comprehensive reference banks and photo files. Often these resources are not open to the public but once you explain you are a freelance writer, permission will be granted to use the facilities. Just one more reason to carry business cards.

Professional organizations are always willing to help a writer. Many are nonprofit enterprises with limited advertising budgets. They depend on word-of-mouth for the donations that keep them alive so they welcome the exposure and are willing to exchange information for acknowledgement.

A good example of this is a piece I did on the Big Brothers. It was included in a larger article focusing on ways to help your community through volunteering. One phone call gave me more pamphlets, answers to questions and quotes than I could possibly use.

Here's where the reference file proved indispensable. I stored everything I didn't need and later wrote a piece about seniors becoming Big Brothers and another on the benefits of the organization from the child's point of view.

Tourist bureaus, everywhere, are one of the best sources of material. They send maps, brochures, files, photography, press releases...anything you could conceivably want. There is no charge, but they do expect credit for the material and return of all photography.

One fax to a Newfoundland tourist agency, inquiring only about the availability of slides for a query I was putting together, brought mounds of material—and many excellent slides.

When requesting photography, be specific in your needs. Be sure you state if you want transparencies (slides), colour or black and white print, and the size. (Writer's guidelines usually state photography requirements.)

Government offices are cooperative when asked for assistance in specialized areas. They have helped me with everything from witness support services to harassment in the work place. One ministry faxed me pages of material, followed by posted originals. They didn't want to delay my work while the mail took its time getting to me.

Most organizations see education as a prime objective so when you contact them for assistance you can be sure you will get it.

The same holds true for many companies. I was searching for the ingredients in Buttermilk Paint, a favourite decorating compound of my grandparents. I called every paint company I could think of and, finally, one gave me the address of a company in the mid-western United States which still make the product. I wrote, explaining my writing project, and within a few days had the history of the paint, the recipe, how it's used today...everything.

Good public relations are foremost in their minds. One word of caution. Depending on the subject, the point of view may be slanted in the company's favour. It's up to you to sort out all material and perhaps check it further with neutral authorities. If the topic is controversial, contact both sides and report fairly.

Many experts, in a variety of disciplines, are open to the freelance writer. Frequently, I seek direction from the medical profession. I have never been turned away.

Including comments from respected authorities gives weight to your writing. Don't be afraid to approach them. This can be done by a phone call requesting an appointment (some prefer to just talk to you on the phone) or by a letter introducing yourself.

I have heard journalists say they "threaten" professionals who refuse an interview by telling them they will print, "Mr. X was unco-operative when asked for a statement", thereby putting him in a bad light. Usually, they get the meeting—and a lot of hard feelings as well.

I don't believe in this kind of approach. It is the individual's right to refuse comment and you should respect that. If you have been pleasant and professional, and still he wishes not to comply, go elsewhere.

I was doing an article on animal health care and asked a veterinarian for his help. Although I knew him well, he didn't want to do it but, because I was polite and patient, he put me in touch with one who did. Had I been aggressive, I wouldn't have talked to anyone.

Working with professionals can be fun. When I needed step-by-step photographs of grooming a cat, I borrowed one of my neighbour's felines and trotted it off to the local pet care centre.

It was quite a day. That cat did not want to be groomed—he was doing just fine on his own, thank you very much. We have pictures of all the stages: the flattened ears, the suds, the airborne cat. It sold the first time out.

Occasionally, an article will require a number of opinions and one of the ways to obtain them is through survey. This can be time consuming so if you have a two week deadline, don't attempt it.

Send out twice as many forms as you need. Keep them to one page each and as simple as possible so that they are uncomplicated to fill out. Be sure to include a SASE because, if you don't, your chances of reply are slim at best.

You need to be organized to conduct a survey, from deciding whom you want to poll to how you want to do it. Are you going to use the mail? Deliver door to door? What about the bylaws in your area?

Obviously, you are not going to do this for a 500 word article but if you are assigned a feature with a major magazine, it may be worth the time and expense.

A simpler way to gather opinions is to write a letter to the editor. Explain who you are, what material/information you need and why, and include your address and phone number. The response will surprise you.

Some of your best research will be conducted in your own files. If you have set up a workable system and not tossed everything in a drawer, you will have much of what you need at your fingertips.

Your assignment is to write about an exotic honeymoon destination. The editor is open to ideas but would like the focus to be somewhere in the tropics. Let's have a look at your files.

You started out with one general file—travel. As it grew unmanageable you separated it into locations, ie: North America, Tropical, Europe, etc. These again were broken down into subcategories.

You want exotic destinations so you pull the files that divided from TROPICAL: Hawaii, Caribbean, etc. For our example, we'll use Hawaii.

The Hawaii files are divided into Beach Resorts, Hotels, Shopping, Restaurants, Bridal/Honeymoon Packages, Tours...and so on. Obviously, you'll start with the Bridal/Honeymoon file but you also have other material that would interest a traveller, honeymoon or not, at your fingertips. This information will add depth and mood to the finished piece.

Make sure you keep all your notes, tapes, letters...everything! I don't think there's a safe time to throw them out. You have no idea when you are going to be asked to back up a statement or prove a source.

The only unpleasant incident I've ever had in my writing life was saved from becoming a court case because I could prove it was bad editing on the part of the magazine and not my research.

The sentence in my original manuscript had quoted, from source material supplied by the city, the upper and lower prices of property. The editor, severely cutting my article, removed the upper figure therefore giving the impression that beach front was selling for way below market value. The Town Hall was inundated with calls!

When questioned, I faxed my original work and copies of the source material to the Chamber of Commerce of the municipality involved and to the publisher of the magazine, with copies to the editor. The periodical's retraction completely vindicated me.

There's something to be said for the magazine that sends galleys (drafts of the finished article) for you to proof read. Had this been the case, I would have picked up the error and saved everyone a lot of trouble.

This occurred several months after the article came out. If I had decided there was no use keeping backup of published material, I would have been sued. KEEP EVERYTHING— even if that means renting a storage locker, at some point. Computer disks makes storage files much simpler to manage but I still keep hard copy (paper).

Retrieving your research can be as easy as you make it. No matter how good your material is, it's useless unless you can get at it.

Right from the first day, develop the habit of filing in an orderly manner and do it as soon as you have something to save. If you let the paper grow into an unruly pile, the chances of proper storage grow less as the stack grows higher.

Small clippings from newspapers and magazines can become lost. I attach them to a piece of paper the same size as my files and label the top. Many clippings on the same subject can fill one piece of paper.

Large envelopes can also be used to hold thematic clippings. These are labelled and filed in folders. For example: your main file is ANIMALS. Inside the folder are envelopes labelled, dogs, cats, rabbits, horses, animal health, pet grooming, and so on. When you need specific information, it's easily retrieved.

Another method is to file all information alphabetically. For this, cross reference in a card index is a necessity and a numbered filing system must be set up.

Your ANIMALS file would no longer exist. Dogs would be under D, cats C, etc. Lets pull Dogs. Page one is labelled D-001 and is information on seeing-eye dogs. Page 2, D-002, has reference material on ear mites.

The alphabetically arranged card index would contain the corresponding subject (ear mites, under E) and its location in the main files, and would be cross referenced with a card labelled DOG. This card lists all the topics dealing with dogs and the location in the files.

This may seem cumbersome to set up but it is a very efficient programme. If you are just starting a filing system, the work load will be manageable, growing as you grow.

Cross reference with computer files is advisable. If you are working in WINDOWS, use the card file in your programme. If you are in a DOS programme, create a file. Backup on disk.

Never make computer files your only source of reference. Things like crashes (complete loss of material) can happen. Also, there are times when you need to access the file without exiting the programme. Hard copy can be pulled and information used while you are writing.

However you store your research, be sure it is an analytical and extendable system that you are comfortable with. The last thing you want to do is spend hours of valuable time hunting and filing!

Collecting sets of information can go a long way in the organization of resource material. Try to keep only those pieces that are unusual or that will add a new dimension to an everyday topic. Never forget, that the facts you are storing have to be those that will lead to a sale.

Your research has turned up a quote you'd like to use in your article. This brings us to the question of permissions.

A general rule of thumb is that you can use facts you've found in printed material but you must not reproduce a paragraph—not even a word for word sentence—without permission from the owner of the copyright. Fine. But how do you tell who owns it?

In the first few pages of the magazine or book you have been using to gather information, is a notice of copyright. Usually, it reads: Copyright Ina Writer, 1994. Generally, the publisher's address will appear underneath. The publisher can, by contract, authorize reprint of excerpts. However, if the author has retained the rights, you will still communicate through the publisher's address.

Write a short letter explaining who you are, what passage you wish to quote and the purpose, including the name of the publication slated to carry the excerpt. I usually wait until the article is accepted before requesting permissions.

It is unlikely that a publisher or author will get upset if you quote a few words and attribute the source but, if you start getting into entire pages or even paragraphs, write for permission.

There may be a charge back to the copyright holder, similar to royalties, so make sure you understand the terms of the permissions granted.

This is a very important part of your research as every piece of material is copyright as soon as it's on paper...even your letters to friends. Information and ideas cannot be made copyright, only the method by which they are expressed.

You are at liberty to use data you find in any published work providing it is presented in an entirely different structure. You must make all ideas your own. Copyright will be dealt with in detail in a further chapter.

THE INTERVIEW

Perhaps the single most important asset for a writer is the ability to conduct a good interview. From one successful interview you will have enough information to write several articles, all with a different focus. The technique can be learned. It is simply a candid conversation in which you are trying for the sum total of a personality.

There is nothing to be nervous about so never let yourself be intimidated by your own imagination.You have the edge. The person on the receiving end of the questions is talking about a topic dear to him... himself.

Go into an interview prepared. Read everything you can find that's been written about your subject. Talk to his friends, business associates, family. Look for little-known facts and inconsistencies.

Be subjective enough to identify with him and objective enough to explain him reliably to the reader.

This holds true, not only for the personal profile, but for the interview conducted to gain expert comment.

There seem to be stages both parties go through as an interview progresses. At first, there is a certain amount of nervousness, perhaps even suspicion, while each begins to "know" the other.

As you relax, you are given greater insight into his personality and his particular talent. You begin to identify with some of the things that are being said.

You may find you are beginning to enjoy your subject and you start concentrating on all the positive aspects of his character. Don't lose sight of the fact that a good interview is balanced. Seek the bad as well as the good. It is the only positive way to a well-rounded image...even if you don't use the material.

You may be tempted to push your subject in the direction you wish the interview to take. Don't. Be a good listener with the ability to lead.

As the interview continues, a rapport will develop. This is when you will acquire your best quotes and see the complete personality. End the interview on an "up" note and leave your subject with a feeling of having accomplished something worthwhile.

Guard against bias. To prejudge is to be prejudiced. You want your reader to trust you.

HOW TO CONDUCT AN INTERVIEW

You are prepared. You have read the research profile until you know it so well you seldom have to refer to your notes. You have set up a comfortable environment for yourself and your subject because you have reduced the formality of "interview" to the relaxed state of conversation.

Choose a location that's equally as comfortable. I dislike interviewing in public places, such as restaurants, although it is sometimes necessary. I prefer the subject's office/home because he is on his turf and is more apt to be calm and talkative. If it is a professional setting, such as a classroom, you have the added advantage of seeing his work.

Be on time, dressed in a businesslike fashion. Too early and you catch him unprepared, setting the wrong tone for the interview. The same applies if you are late. His time is valuable...he sees it as more valuable than yours. If your appointment is for 2 PM, you be there at 2 PM!

If you have permission to use a tape recorder, bring plenty of blank cassettes. Make sure the recorder is unobtrusive and placed where it is least likely to interfere with concentration.

Tape recorders are the best way to gather material. There is no question later about what he said or how he said it. There is no danger of misquoting.

It took me a long time to get used to using a tape recorder but now I don't like to use anything else. It sets the scene for simple, friendly conversation and allows you to gather all knowledge the subject has to offer.

Tapes are easily filed for future reference. One of my first experiences with an interviewee was a professional who insisted he "hadn't said that" when he saw his words in print. One quick listen to the tape stopped any chance of an argument. Words do look different when they're published!

Make sure you get permission to use gathered information for further articles. Tapes can contain varied topics and you never know when you'll want to use them.

In today's busy world, telephone interviews are becoming routine. They are not as good as face to face meetings but they do have their place.

An assignment made it necessary for me to interview a couple in Beverly Hills, CA. Obviously, flying to Los Angles, while it would have been nice, was impractical and a telephone interview took place.

The same rules apply. Be prepared. Possibly, preparedness is even more important on the phone than in person. You can't pause to look through notes or sip coffee and, at cost per minute, you don't want to stray from the subject.

Most answering machines are able to record conversations. If yours does not, try to get one that does. Calls from editors, questions on submissions, receiving editorial direction, are only a few of the reasons, besides interviews, why the machine is a necessity in a writer's office.

Develop your telephone voice because it is the only link you have with your subject. Be clear and confident, keep the tone low and pleasant, and be aware of using inflection. Practise on your friends.

After the phone interview is completed, send the final draft and the form stating the quotes are correct to the person you interviewed. Have him check the facts and return the signed form. When the article is printed, don't forget to send a copy.

To readily access interview material, set up a card or computer file for your numbered tapes. Write the general subject on the tape and a detailed account of the topics it covered on the index card. Do this soon after you complete the interview so all information is clear in your mind.

If you must take notes, take them while the interview is in progress. I've heard writers say they don't like to stop the subject from talking while they "catch up" (another plus for a recorder) so they wait until they get home to make notes.

I would like to know how they do that! It would terrify me to have to rely on memory, even minutes later, to reproduce a perfectly accurate quote. Nor would I like to have to phone the subject to verify information.

The first few minutes of the interview will set the pace and form the subject's opinion of you. Make the most of it. This time also allows you to "read" the interviewee. If he is an egotist, he will respond to praise while an introvert will mistrust it—and you.

Try to find a common interest to begin the conversation. Has he paintings or furnishings you are familiar with? What about pets, children, hobbies? Humour, if you're good at it, helps break the ice.

Above all, be interested in what he is telling you. If you stop listening, he'll stop talking.

Never interrupt him with a question. You'll find that many of the things you want to ask will be answered in general conversation. Ask questions only if there is a lull in the conversation or if he is getting terribly off-track and time is running short.

Try to get an exclusive for at least three months.

This way, he will not talk to anyone else and the chances of your story showing up in a competing publication are slim.

Before you leave, make another appointment with him to read your manuscript before submission. There are conflicting opinions surrounding this practice but I never give anything to an editor that has not been cleared by the person I interviewed. I want the protection of having him read the copy and check the quotes, with the understanding that the exact printed version may differ slightly.

Newspapers often have hard and fast rules against this procedure. It's based on the principle that a reader could question the article's authenticity if he knew the subject interviewed had "veto" power over what was or wasn't printed.

It is good policy to have the interviewee sign a cover letter to your editor that indicates he has seen the final draft and agrees with your account of his facts and quotes, and that he understands some editing will take place.

Develop the practice of carrying these forms in your briefcase. Draw up a simple letter on your computer:

Dear......(editor)

I have read the final draft of........(title), by......

(your name) and agree that all facts and quotes are correct as I stated them. I also understand that editing of the copy may be necessary but that the meaning will remain as I intended.

Sincerely,

...............(name of interviewee)   DATE.......

When the article is published, be sure you send a copy to the person who assisted you with a thank you note for the interview.

WRITING THE INTERVIEW

The most important thing about writing an interview is to do it as soon after the session as you possibly can.

It doesn't matter that you have everything on tape, you will not fully capture the personality of your subject if you leave it—even for a day or two. There are things that shine in an interview, things you carry away with you, and they stay for a very short period of time.

Write the first draft. Don't try for sentence structure or flawless spelling. Try for all those little things you picked up that gave colour and roundness to your subject.

You do this by keeping the images in mind. If, for example, you think of his dress or something about the surroundings, write it in. Later editing can always remove it. It is this first draft that will capture the whole person.

You must act as an intermediary between your reader and the interviewee. He has something to say and you want it to be a real person who is saying it. If you fail to do this, your interview is nothing more than a boring succession of quotes.

You want to enrich your reader. One of the most profound interviews I did was with a long time friend who was dying of cancer. The illness was progressing rapidly but he had such a sense of himself that he left me with a feeling of acceptance and peace.

"It's okay...I don't fear death," he'd said, quietly when I'd tried to tell him I was sorry. "At this point in my life, I've accepted the existence of a plan in the universe. There is order. I'm coming to life, again."

That statement, with its many facetted meaning, has stayed with me as I'm sure it has with those who read it.

Your first draft is completed and, reading it over, you know you have captured the person. It says everything you want it to say. In fact, it is probably the best thing you've ever written! Now put it away.

There is a phenomenon that happens to writers. We fall in love with our own work. Like lovers, we overlook the flaws. We concentrate on all the brilliance. It is imperative that you put the draft away for a day or two—or however long it takes you to "cool off".

Difficult if you have a deadline but something you absolutely must do! When you return to the work, you will proceed with the editing in an objective manner. Play with the structure and never forget you are telling a story. Stories are entertaining. Rearrange your quotes. Vary the tone. Read it aloud, over and over, to make sure the flow is smooth. If you stumble, there is something wrong with your writing.

Check your manuscript to be certain you have established a time frame. The article may be reprinted years later and your reader must have a reference point.

Equally as important, is giving your reader a visual image of the person. In context, bring out a physical feature, a side of his personality, an event that shaped his life. This is the round out your character statement that crops up in editor's rejection letters. It means, give him life.

Keep your copy fresh (original) by staying away from trite expressions and overworked phrases. This brings up the question of reproducing quotes.

What do you do when a person makes a glaring grammatical error? Do you leave the error or do you change the quote? What about the long-winded answer to a question. Have you the right to cut it and risk changing the meaning?

I do what's required to write a good article, being extremely careful to stay true to the intent. This is another argument for letting the interviewee see the copy. You can point out cuts and changes in sentence structure—changes your editor is sure to make if you don't. Reading the article before it goes to print and signing the form that the facts are correct, keeps everyone happy.

Your aim is to guide your reader on an examination of what the subject said. You never draw conclusions and you never force your views. You might disagree to the point that you refuse an assignment, but you never use an interview as a soapbox.

To summarize:
1. Research your material and your subject.
2. Set your interview in a place comfortable to both.

3. Be on time and be professional.

4. Use conversation rather than question. Let him talk. Record whenever you can.

5. Be objective and never intimidate.

6. Collect more material then you need.

7. Leave the interviewee with a positive feeling.

Strive for the well-balanced interview, one that tells of both successes and failures. Getting people to open up is an art, one that you will perfect with practice. Try out your skills on those you live with and ask for an honest appraisal. Accept criticism with grace.

If your subject becomes argumentative, change the subject. If he talks above you, explain that you are just a lay person, as are the readers of the magazine. Done right, he will take this as the highest form of compliment and give you material everyone can understand.

Ask questions about everything you don't understand. If you make a mistake during an interview, admit it. Never try to bluff your way out—you are dealing with an expert.

Guard against invasion of privacy. If someone says, "It's off the record"...it's off the record! You only need to break a confidence once to destroy everything you've worked for.

Respect his right to life. If in doubt, ask what he will or will not be comfortable with seeing in print. Public revelation of facts without permission, even if they are true, can be embarrassing at least. At worst, they can lead to law suits.

THE HOME RESEARCH LIBRARY

Setting up a good reference library will be an ongoing part of your writing life. Space will dictate what you can keep in your office. If you have an entire wall of shelves, you are to be envied.

Keep at hand those books which you use every day. You'll soon know what they are. Have some place, even if it is another part of the house, where all other reference books are easily obtainable. Nothing is more frustrating than trying to find some bit of resource material.

I have mentioned the way to acquire good books. Just to summarize: be familiar with the book before you purchase it; ask for books you want for birthdays, Christmas, etc; watch second-hand stores, garage sales, friend's discards; join book clubs; subscribe to proven writer's magazines.

Try to set your library up by category so that all information on one subject is readily available. Have a few books that are brief fact sources. Three I have come to mind and all of them are READER'S DIGEST publications: North American Wildlife, Illustrated Encyclopedic Dictionary, How in the World. Others are Bartletts Familiar Quotations, The Reverse Dictionary, and several books on usage.

A HOME VIDEO LIBRARY is also valuable. There are many subjects on the public television stations, as well as the open learning courses, that supply you with a ready source of information.

I have volumes of tapes on animals, psychology, history, art, people profiles, poetry, children's literature...and on and on.

I try to keep similar subjects on one tape. When the TV Guide arrives for the next week, I go through it carefully and mark everything that could be of interest for my library.

Again, we are not talking about copying the material—we are talking about reference for fact collecting.

One last word before we leave research—CHECK YOUR SOURCES AND YOUR FACTS. Never assume, because someone has told you they are expert, that they know what they're talking about.

You certainly hope they do. But, don't take the chance. If you can't verify it—don't use it.

CHAPTER EIGHT

WRITING THE ARTICLE

You get up early, your head bursting with ideas. All night long, you've been composing sentences and building word patterns to rival the world's best. The accepted query has filled you with confidence and you just know the article you are going to write will be award winning stuff.

Coffee's poured, the paper is in the typewriter or the computer is turned on. And guess what happens? Your mind goes blank! Don't feel bad. All over the world there are writers of long standing in exactly the same situation.

Some days are worse than others. There are times when the blank paper phenomenon lasts only a few minutes. But there are times when it won't go away.

The best thing you can do is write. Remove from your mind any notion that what you put on the paper or screen is engraved in stone. I guarantee it will be changed—and probably more than once.

One of the things I find helpful is writing the first paragraph or two with pencil and paper. There is something less permanent, and therefore less threatening, about words that can be erased.

You must plan ahead. Organize your research so that's it's readily available and in order of events as they happened. Discard all facts that are not related and avoid the mundane. One of the best ways to establish order is to have an outline.

Jot down on a piece of paper the sequence of information. For example, your article is on finding a child given up for adoption. Your outline would look something like this:

1. Introduce the parent who is searching. Give the background.

2. Use her quotes about the pregnancy.

3. Talk about the birth and the adoption. Use quotes to support this.

4. A section on her feelings about the separation from her daughter and coping with the grieving period.

5. Cover the years between the adoption and the search.

6. How/why the search began. quotes).

7. How her husband and family are coping.

8. Information on the organizations that are helping. Include the "red tape" involved.

9. Tell how/when the child was found. Use quotes here for expression of feeling, etc.

10. Quotes from other members of the family.

11. Summarize by saying where the mother/daughter are now in their relationship, what they expect from the future and end with a strong quote.

12. Sidebars (informational inserts) will hold statistical data.

It is unlikely that you will stay 100 percent to the outline. It will change and shift as you get into the article. It will change even more with the editing. However, it does act as a security blanket each time you feel the whole thing is getting out of hand.

A general outline that works for most articles and can act as a guide when formulating the topical framework, follows.

1. Get the reader's attention by using a quote, anecdote or contrasting points of view.

2. State the problem.

3. Involve the reader in the problem.

4. Use the drama of detail to involve the reader further and force him to begin forming his own opinions. Include examples with which the reader can identify.

5. Give some conflicting facts to widen the point of view and make the reader question his convictions.

6. Prod the reader into resolving his conflicts.

There are a few things you must always keep in mind. In nonfiction, you do not want to make your reader guess what you mean. Spell it out. With impact. If the article calls for a forceful presentation, then be forceful. Pick up the mood of the topic.

It is a good idea to give your first draft a working title. (Titles will be discussed later in the chapter.) As your work load increases, you are apt to find yourself writing several things at the same time. While this is far from an ideal situation, it happens. The reason—deadlines.

Working titles that identify pages let you shift, as time dictates, without risk of mixing content. They also make computer files easy to access when you retrieve the copy.

The only thing you need for a working title is a few words. Back to the woman looking for her daughter. CHILD FIND would do nicely. Keep it short and type it on every page. You might have first drafts of several articles printed out for editing.

Before you start the actual writing of the article, you must decide whether you want to write First Person, or Third Person narrative.

Many of us were taught that First Person, the use of "I", was a poor approach to a story. A myth. It is an effective way of handling an article, especially when you find yourself relating events that are out of the ordinary.

First Person narrative helps to bring the reader into the experience. It is the best method for travel articles, exposes, and adventure stories.

Third Person is used when you want the reader in a spectator role. While usually used in fiction, it can be effective in nonfiction as well.

You approach the article as if you were going to write a short story. To do this you must have characters (profile) to develop and a plot with a climax. Without these elements, you can't write third person narrative because you are in a straightforward, first person reporting situation.

Now, you are ready to begin your article. Don't worry about word count or tense or spelling. Get your ideas down. Let them flow. Say everything you want to say because editing is going to happen.

Refer to your outline and start at:

THE BEGINNING

It is very important to have a hook (a paragraph that captures your reader's attention). If the opening of your article is dull, it is unlikely to be read.

There are five effective entries:

1. The Statement. example: Sarah was 22, unmarried and pregnant. It was a time when society shunned unwed mothers and babies were signed away with the knowledge they would never be seen again.

LOST AND FOUND, Western People/ 29 July 1993

2. The Question. example: Have you any idea what's it's like travelling with a drunk and disorderly cat?

THE PILL, THE CARIBBEAN & THE CAT, I Love Cats Nov/89

3. The Quotation. example: "Rituals are milestones—they mark a journey. They are not the journey." Barbara Desforges, from her interview for LIFETIME PROMISES, Our Family/ July 1992

4. The Anecdote. example: We were only four hours into retirement and suddenly our marriage had serious problems. I don't know what I'd expected...probably peace, contentment and leisure time. What I got was a whole new meaning to the word responsibility.

RETIREMENT FOXTROT, Our Family/September 1988

5. The Alarm. example: If you are a parent coping with an alcoholic child, you must have the strength and the love to do one thing—stop helping him.

FAITH AND RECOVERY, Recovery Today/April 1991

Your choice of opening will have a lot to do with the type of market for which you are writing. Whichever one you use, it should involve the reader, draw him into wanting to read further, and tell him something new and interesting.

Opening paragraphs are short. They are catchy. They use the word "you" whenever possible (a trick to involve the reader) and they introduce the subject. An editor is often persuaded to read the article because you were able to pique his curiosity. If the first paragraph lets him down, it could mean rejection.

A common fault is to leave the introduction of the topic until the second or third paragraph. Novice writers think this is a way of building suspense; to make the reader continue just to find out what they are talking about.

Don't fall into this trap. You only have a few words to work with so cram as much information in as quickly as you can and move on to:

THE MIDDLE

You have succeeded in seizing your reader's attention. Now, you have to keep it. The body of your article must not read like a roster of fact, a reference book, or a brochure. This might be nonfiction but you are still telling a story.

Lists of statistics are written in sidebars. These are compact bits of information, contained within the article in "boxes" at the end or side of the main piece. I attach a separate sheet of paper for each, submitted along with the manuscript.

example:

SIDEBAR ONE

1. Residents pay income tax as follows: 3% on the first $2,500.; 6% on the next $5,000; 10% on the next $7,500; 15% on the next $10,000; and 20% on all income exceeding $25,000.

2. Taxes are imposed on gross income from all sources.

3. No tax credit is given for personal allowances.

SIDEBAR TWO

Thoroughbred Breeding Costs

1. Training fees average $1000 per month

2. Boarding costs average $250 per month for winter months and $10 per day when racing.

3. Stud fees begin at $1000.

4. There are costs incurred for: vets, transportation of the mare, feed, farrier, insurance, registration.

You can easily see that, while this information is relevant, it would be difficult to write into context without being extremely dull. Sidebars can handle, in a few words, all statistics you need to cover.

The body of your article contains the information. Try to include as many little known facts as you can. You want to leave your reader with the feeling that he's learned something valuable and that he's had a good time doing it.

Talk to your reader. I see the work of novice writers whose sentences scream Thesaurus. I read the sentence out loud then ask them to tell me what they mean. Their expression, in words, is likely to be the one they should have written.

Assemble your facts in a series of interesting stories. Use comparisons. Stay away from all the trite modifiers: very big, really nice, lovely. You do have to say how big, how nice, etc. but the words you chose will give tone and depth to your story.

example:

It was the expanse of the area that struck me. Even from the air, it was obvious that a good-sized city could have been dropped into the space without filling it.

This passage illustrates comparison and qualifiers. Reread your work and always ask yourself if there is a better way to say it.

If you have not been able to assemble enough anecdotal material then create your own. There is nothing wrong with using correlation. After all, an anecdote is nothing more than life experience told in story form. What you can't do is pass your experience off as someone else's, and you must never "invent" facts.

An example of augmenting a story is one I wrote about my grandparents settling on a Southern Alberta farm. My grandfather had come from Hungary when he was in his late teens. After several years alone, he decided he needed a wife, wrote the parents of a child he remembered on a neighbouring Hungarian farm, and "bought" my grandmother, sight unseen.

She was sent to North America by steerage when she was 13, with nothing except a small basket that contained her life. I did have all the facts because my grandmother told me about her experiences over the years. But the article was written after her death so her thoughts and feelings were a creation compiled from my memory and the reactions that would have been hers.

Quotations also give life to an article but there is a skill in using them effectively. New writers want to "string them together" as an easy way of completing the piece. Nothing will lose your reader's attention faster than an unbroken list of quotes!

Stagger them with description or background narrative. For example:

Some expectant mothers only need an occasional sounding-board, so a phone call is enough. JUST FOR MOMS companions are there right through the first six weeks after the birth.

"The six weeks after delivery is a difficult time," Laurie points out. "Hormones are out of whack. Suddenly, there's this little person that comes with no manual."

Laurie puts both clients and companions through an extensive screening.....

"My own mother doesn't know I'm pregnant..."

JUST FOR MOMS, B.C. Woman to Woman November 1993

There is a great deal of descriptive material between these quotes. Had this not been done, my article would have sounded like a testimonial.

Another common mistake is the writer interjecting with he told me..., I asked..., etc. No one wants to hear about you. The transitions must be smooth.

The following example is from THE HOME STRETCH, Focus on Women January 1991.

In 1965, Judy married. They moved to Vancouver Island in 1973 and bought a two acre farm in North Saanich.

"It wasn't much," Judy said. "There was a ramshackle barn and a few outbuildings—even the house needed work...."

The incorrect way to handle this quote would have been: I asked Judy about the farm. "It wasn't much," she told me....

Quotations reflect the views of other people. They make it easier for the reader to identify with the problems and opinions being expressed by the writer.

There are other sources of quotes than those gleaned from personal interview. What about the "famous person" quotes that we all see as leads and support material? You can re-quote from interviews published elsewhere, from research articles, from books of quotations, such as BARTLETTS FAMILIAR QUOTATIONS.

One word of caution—if you are using more than a sentence or two, write for permission. And, always credit your source.

Constructing the body of your article deserves special attention. Think past the content. Style, mood, and voice must be considered.

The style is something that will develop naturally. Don't try to pattern your work after someone you admire and don't consciously set out to develop a technique. Let the words flow. Write what you feel. That's your style.

Mood can often be taken from the context of the article. Obviously, if you are writing a story about abuse, you will not treat it with humour. In most cases, the act of writing in accordance with the topic, will automatically produce the desired mood.

The voice of the article is more complex. It comes from the voice of the verb—active or passive. The ACTIVE voice indicates that the subject of a sentence is performing or causing an ACTION. This action is expressed by the verb.

For instance: The dog chases the rabbit. The dog (subject) is performing the action. This action, chasing, is shown through the verb, chases.

The PASSIVE voice indicates that the subject of the sentence is the object of the action or the effect of the verb....something has something done to it.

Back to the dog and the rabbit. If the sentence reads: The rabbit is being chased by the dog, it is passive voice.

The subject (rabbit) is the recipient or object of the action...being chased. The sentence does not tell us what something is doing but what is being done to it.

Voice is something you must understand. If this is confusing you, read it over and over. Practise until you understand it.

Editors favour the ACTIVE voice because it is more direct. Less words are needed to say the same thing. It's a good idea to read several magazine and newspaper articles until it becomes second nature to recognize the voice...and then make it a habit to write in the active voice. You will save yourself many rejections.

The first draft of the body is complete. You are satisfied that you've worked in all your facts and used your quotations effectively. Now it's time to think about:

THE ENDING

The closing paragraphs are almost as important as your opening. You will find editors who read the beginning and the end, skipping all the meat in the middle.

The theory is, if you can grab your reader in the first sentences and leave him feeling satisfied in the last, then what's in the middle has to be good. There's truth in this.

What you want to avoid at all cost is just stopping. If you do this, you give your reader the impression that you ran out of information and didn't know where to go. Your ability is questioned.

You are aiming for a paragraph that closes with impact so save some of your best material until the end. An emotion-laden quote, a vivid description, a surprise conclusion—all are effective.

Good closing paragraphs also summarize the article. Your reader must feel complete. He has been drawn into forming a conclusion and he's enjoyed it.

He'll look forward to reading more of your work.

The first draft completed, the process of falling in love with your work begins. Print it out and put it away for a day or two. You can use this time of head clearing to begin another article, send out queries, check your files and card index, clear out the office.

When you feel you can be objective, take out the first draft and start editing.

There is nothing mystical about editing your own work. You just have to be ruthless. I find it necessary to see the work on paper to get a feel for the printed piece. Somehow, everything looks better on the computer screen than it really is.

I double or triple space my first draft so that I can rewrite on the manuscript. If I want to add more, I number the line and add the addition or revision on the back.

Take out every word that's not necessary to the story. I don't mean removing every adjective and adverb but I do mean removing some of them!

One of the most common mistakes made by beginners is the overuse of adjectives. Select the ones you do use with care. Make sure they say exactly what you want them to say...and ask yourself if the sentence has improved because they are there.

The adjective must be directly connected to a noun and its purpose is to enhance the word picture or clarify a meaning. The following sentence is dreadful, It was a very big, rosy red, full flower that graced the plant.

You have a plant with a beautiful flower and you want your sentence to do it justice. The red flower was exquisite, so lush it weighed down the plant.

You have said the same thing. Both sentences tell you what it is, how big it is and what it looks like.

Your first draft was a statement of ideas. The second draft is for house cleaning. You must pay attention to punctuation, not only because the editor may judge you as a sloppy writer if you don't, but because misplaced marks can change the meaning.

There are a few main rules governing the use of punctuation. Take a minute to learn them.

1. A period, semicolon and colon have the same purpose. They divide sections of connected thought. In all cases where a semicolon is used a period could have been substituted. Then why use a semicolon at all?

A period makes two separate sentences stand on their own while a semicolon links parallel expressions more closely together. The one you choose will give a slightly different cast to the meaning. Let's take a look at an example:

The company owns vast potato, cabbage and corn plantings. It imports machinery from all over the world.

or

The company owns vast potato, cabbage and corn plantings; it imports machinery from all over the world.

It is really a matter of preference because the meaning remains unchanged.

A colon is always used when one sentence introduces another sentence. It was the first thing I did: I locked the door.

The colon brings you to a full stop and is often used to introduce drama in your story. It is also used to separate a list. I looked over the wall and saw: roses, asters, poppies and an abundance of vines running wild.

One typing space is left between the semicolon and the words it connects. ...corn plantings; it imports... Two spaces are left between the colon or the period, and the words they connect.—plantings. It imports... or ...I did: I locked...

2. A comma is the briefest pause in all punctuation. One use is to separate parts of a sentence to clarify the meaning.

The Liberals, say the Conservatives, are sure to win the next election has a vastly different meaning than The Liberals say the Conservatives are going to win the next election.

It is used to separate nonrestrictive terms (additional information that can be left out of the sentence without altering the meaning). For example: In my article, SHOES, I stated... The word shoes can be removed without destroying the thought.

COMMAS:

enclose phrases inserted into a sentence. The dress, because it was a neutral shade, was easy to accessorize.

enclose phrases that have a common element but express only one. It is the best, if not the only, red car on the lot.

are used between Coordinate Clauses—long clauses with different thoughts. The tree was planted six years ago, but the flowers underneath were put in this year. These clauses are introduced with but, not, nor, or, neither, and.

are used between Subordinate Clauses and long phrases that precede the Principal Clause. They are introductory phrases or clauses. If too many of the stores closed on Sunday, the tax revenue would drop considerably.

enclose inserted words or phrases. Of course, indeed, nevertheless, actually.

are used when however, therefore, etc. begin the sentence.

are used after a short phrase of thinking. Those shoes are too big, I think.

are used after a short phrase that denotes a question. That was the right road, wasn't it?

are used before a quotation. Jimmy said, "I will go with you."

One of the most common errors is using a comma in place of a colon. The manager had another memo for his employees this week, the long awaited news of a raise.

Another mistake is using a comma in place of a semicolon. Not only can he dance, he dances professionally. This requires a longer pause than the comma allows.

When a comma is used in place of a period (full stop), the result is a run-on sentence. I ran down the road, it was too early for school, but I knew I could play on the swings. Obviously, there should have been a period after road.

Other uses for the comma, such as enclosing proper names, after yes and no, etc. are straightforward and should not be confusing to you. If you find you are still unsure of usage, arm yourself with a CLEARLY WRITTEN book on punctuation.

3. Dashes are useful when separating nonessential phrases from the rest of the sentence. They are an excellent dramatic tool when not over used. Written in the manuscript, they should be —, rather than one -, which can be confused with a hyphen. He sat at the back of the room—as he later told me—to ward off the prying eyes of strangers.

Brackets could have replaced the dash but they are usually used to insert information into a sentence. Sentence structure is most important (detailed later in the chapter) and should be given your closest attention.

4. Hyphens should be used only when absolutely necessary to clarify the meaning of the sentence. Take the sentence, The fund provides for nursing home care. What does that mean?

If written nursing home care, it is care at home by nurses. If written nursing-home care, it is care in a nursing home. Make sure what you write is what you mean.

One of the essentials in your home library is a good book on English usage. Purchase it carefully because you are buying something to help you. It is no good to you if it's so technical that you can't understand it.

Let's have a look at the stages in editing. This excerpt is the beginning of an article written for SIMPLY SENIORS.

FIRST DRAFT
So...you've given up beef in your diet. Are you sure? The Beef Information Centre reports that just less than one half of the animal is used for meat.

Beef hide is tanned and used as leather for handbags, suitcases, shoes, footballs. The coarse hair of the hide is used for insulation and rugs; the fine hair from the ear for art brushes....

This, again was edited. The lead was weak and needed a hook.

Somewhere between the wrinkles and the middle age spread comes an awareness of health. We all sit down, at one time or the other, and examine our lifestyle. Health is in! Red meat is out!

So...you've given up beef. Are you sure? Reports from the Beef Information Centre suggest that less than half of the animal is used for retail cuts of meat. Fine! you say. This doesn't involve you. You have nothing to do with the byproducts—those things like kidney, liver, tongue and tripe. Those things called offal. Pronounced awful...and rightly so.

In addition to the retail cuts, the offal uses another 5% of the carcass. Guess what? We have half the animal left.

So what about the other edible byproducts? Some margarine and shortenings have their base in beef fats. It is also used in chewing gum and candies. Beef tallow provides the glycerine for some cosmetics, cough syrups, toothpaste, soap, shampoo, detergents.

Bones and horns aren't discarded either. They supply the gelatine for marshmallows, ice cream, canned meats, and pectin. Non-edible gelatine is used in film, wallpaper, glue, toothbrushes, violin strings.

Beef hide is tanned and used as leather for handbags, suitcases, shoes, footballs. The coarse hair of the hide is used for insulation and rugs; the fine hair from the ear for art brushes....

The final copy read:

Somewhere before the wrinkles and after the middle-aged spread, comes an awareness of our own mortality. We all sit down, at one time or another, to examine our lifestyle. The conclusion: health is in; red meat is out!

You've given up beef and you're proud of it. Are you sure you have? Reports from the Beef Information Centre suggests that less than half the animal is used for retail cuts of meat—so where is the rest of it?

Byproducts! you exclaim. They have nothing to do with me. No liver or kidney, tongue nor tripe, will ever pass these lips! Those things are called offal, pronounced awful...and rightly, so.

The offal only takes up another 5% of the carcass. Guess what? We're up to one half the beef that you have nothing to do with. Fifty percent is sneaking up on you.

Open your fridge. Any margarine or shortening in there? BEEF FATS! They are the base for some of these products, as well as for some chewing gums and candies.

Then we have the glycerine from beef tallow showing up in a variety of cosmetics, cough medicines, toothpaste, soap, shampoo, detergents.

Bone and horns aren't discarded, either. They supply the gelatine for marshmallow, ice cream, jellied meats, and pectin. Non-edible gelatine is used in photographic film, wallpaper, toothbrushes, violin strings.

Still not convinced? Unless you're wearing plastic or wooden shoes, there's likely a cow attached to your feet. Tanned beef hide is handbags, suitcases, shoes, footballs.

Even the hair is used. Coarse bristles of the hide is in insulation and rugs; the soft bristles of the ears, in art brushes....

Editing can mean the difference between a fairly good article and an outstanding one. You will never write anything that doesn't need to be "tightened up."

This was another of those little editorial comments that drove me crazy when I was trying to break into the market. It's obvious what "tighten up" means but just how does one do that?

Easy. Take out every unnecessary word that doesn't improve your story. If one word will say it, don't use three.

When you feel the polishing is done, read your story aloud. Phrases that looked good on paper may not work when spoken. Vernacular will jump out at you. Those phrases that brought the warm glow of satisfaction could show themselves as literary snobbery.

Think about every word. Ask yourself, if it's essential or is it padding? If it's padding, it goes.

Stay away from words you don't use in everyday life. If you have to look it up, you can bet your reader WON'T and the article will fail.

Opening sentences with I think..., And then...,

Due to...., Because of...., are the worst form of padding.

Make sure the words you use are the ones you mean.

English is a difficult language. Check everything you are unsure of—and that includes spelling.

Don't underline words or phrases you want to emphasize; it marks you as an amateur. Technically, underlined text signals the editor that you want those words printed in italics. This should be reserved for quotes, titles, references and foreign words.

You do not want to polish the life out of your article. The happy balance that makes work tight without killing it, is something you can only achieve with practice.

The final analysis of your work comes when you read it aloud, one last time, and it flows. There is no hesitation and words don't jump out at you. Learn to edit your own work because clean copy stands a much greater chance of being accepted.

Now it's time to choose a title. You might be tempted to put any old thing on the manuscript to identify it. After all, few titles survive an editors pen. Right? Wrong.

Good titles do. They also catch the editor's eye. A title can mean the difference between acceptance and rejection. I've had editors tell me they seldom read further than the title and the first paragraph before forming an opinion.

A great title won't sell a badly written piece but a fairly good article could be rejected because of a bad title.

What makes a good title? It has few words that are put together in an original way. It gives an indication of the content of the article but only teases the reader's interest. It does not reveal too much.

An example of this is a humorous article I did about a mature couple's second marriage. The title, CHILDREN JUST THINK THEY KNOW BEST, piques your interest without telling you so much that your curiosity is destroyed.

There is always the exception and it'll happen about the time you perfect the art. An editor, with a preference for long titles will crop up. We've all seen the self-help books with banners across their covers: MEN WHO LOVE TO HATE THE WOMEN WHO REJECTED THEM WHEN THEY BECAME SUCCESSFUL. This, of course, is not a real title but you get the picture.

So, when you're starting the quest for a suitable title, check the magazine you have targeted and see where they fall. Short? Go short. Wordy? Stretch it out. One word can work. AIDS, says it all.

Titles can be a phrase from your article. COMING TO LIFE AGAIN, was a quote from the piece on cancer. Had I used, COPING WITH CANCER, it would not have been nearly as effective.

A few words that describe the story, such as, SMILE, PRETTY KITTY far surpasses FELINE PERIODONTAL DISEASE, or I WANT TO KNOW MY CHILD, is better than A MOTHER'S STORY.

If you are unable to find anything you like in your text, then start brainstorming. I often do this even if I'm fairly certain I have the title I want to use.

To brainstorm a title, you put something down on paper. The article is about a couple's 25th wedding anniversary. Let's have a look at what we can draw from.

THE ANNIVERSARY

THE SILVER ANNIVERSARY

CELEBRATING 25 YEARS

THE 25 YEAR EVENT

A SILVER EVENT

A STERLING EVENT...the title I settled on.

Try to avoid using "the". It's cumbersome and can make the title appear trite. THE STERLING EVENT is not as fluid as A STERLING EVENT.

What does the title tell you? It's about a celebration that has something to do with either sterling quality or sterling silver.

What it doesn't tell you, and forces you to read to find out, is the event and why sterling is important.

These questions are answered in the first paragraph.

The work is edited and titled. You are certain it's as good as you can make it. You've put it away for a few days, reread it, and you're still happy. You are ready to submit your work.

Your final copy is double spaced, free from spelling, grammatical, and punctuation errors. It is TYPED (or printed out) on 81/2 x 11" 20 lb. white bond paper. Handwritten work won't be read. Each page has your name and a code word from the title in the upper left hand corner (White/event) and is numbered in the upper right hand corner. Always type "end" on the last page.

Don't ever assume your editor has a clear, organized desk. Make it as easy as you can for him to be able to put your work down, have the pages get mixed, and still bring it back together. He will be working on several things at the same time and if you make his job less stressful, you have a better chance of getting read.

Each submission has a cover sheet, even if it's a 150 word filler. This page has the type of work on the upper left hand corner, your name, address, phone/fax number on the upper right. The title and author are centred. The lower left hand corner tells the editor which rights you are offering and the lower right, the word count.

NONFICTION   Ima Writer

                55 5th Street

                Anyplace, Ont.

                A1A 2B2

                (416) 555-5555 Voice

                (416) 555-5511 Fax

A STERLING EVENT

by

Ima Writer

First N. American Serial Rights   783 words

The cover page gives your editor all the information he needs to respond to your submission. The manuscript should not be stapled nor bound. If you feel it necessary to hook your pages together then use a plastic paper clip.

All Submissions must include a SASE (Self addressed stamped envelope). If you want your manuscript returned then you must include a large envelope with the correct postage. I keep computer copies, as well as one hard copy. I don't want the manuscript back (if I know the editor) so I enclose a business sized, addressed and stamped envelope. He can write and tell me if the submission is rejected or accepted. Hopefully, it comes back with a note and a cheque!

I also enclose a postcard, addressed to me, that reads: Your manuscript........(title) arrived in our office......(date). We expect to get back to you.....(date).

I know: a) it got there, b) it will be read,

c) when it's reasonable to contact them if I haven't heard anything.

Word count is something that gave me nightmares. I knew it had to go on the cover page so, for months, I sat down and COUNTED EVERY WORD. If that doesn't put you to sleep, it will certainly do terrible things for your temperament.

Computers count for you. They enable you to put the exact number of words in your manuscript on the cover page. Without a computer, you have two choices. You can count the words in a few lines, average them, and multiply by the number of lines. Most pages have 25 lines. There is an average of 10 words per line X 25 lines = 250 words per page. Multiply that by the number of pages (remember to account for the half pages) and you have the word count.

The second way is to count the words on 4 or 5 pages, average them and multiply by the number of pages.

This way of counting gives you an approximate word count and you must put that on your cover page. ie: approximately 2500 words.

Word count is important. Most publications have a minimum and maximum word count and they're very strict about staying within the guidelines. The cover page information gives them an idea if your article will fit into the editorial content.

The second reason should be even more important to you—your pay cheque. Many magazines pay per word. You want to have a pretty good idea of what you can expect. We'll deal with this in detail in the chapter on the business end of writing.

Margins deserve your attention. The first page should begin half-way down, leaving the top for the editor's instructions to the printer. If you have chapters in your story, then each one begins half-way down a new page. Don't run chapters together.

Always leave side and bottom margins no less than one inch and not more than two inches. Again, the editor uses these spaces for editorial marks.

Never justify the right hand margin (adjusted so it is flush). The editor's eye is trained to scan a page for word count. If you centre the page or make even right hand margins, the word count changes.

Now it's time for mailing. Envelopes large enough to hold your pages without folding are fine for most manuscripts. However, if you are over 50 pages, you should think about placing them in a box.

Editors do read manuscripts that have been folded into smaller envelopes but if you hit them at the end of a busy day, why take the chance of tipping the scales against you? Presentation counts!

The last thing you include is a covering letter. If you are submitting from an accepted query, refer to the dates of correspondence and the working title. Place on the outside of the package, Requested Material, and the title of the article.

If you are making an unsolicited submission, make sure your covering letter includes your profile along with a short synopsis of the article.

You've written, polished, and polished some more. Your work is the best it can possibly be. Send it away and forget about it. Get on with your work.

If it comes back, target another market and send it right back out. If you get it back 10 times, you'd better sit down and reconsider your work. Either you are submitting to the wrong editors or there is something very wrong with your writing.

Hopefully, you will get that letter or phone call telling you it's been accepted. The editor may suggest rewrites. Put away all artistic temperament and listen to what he says. He's had more experience in publishing than you have and he certainly knows the magazine.

If the debated point changes the meaning, you have reason for question. If the change is the editor's preference, be nice...do what he asks. After all, you want more jobs to come your way.

You want to establish that treasured writer/editor working relationship!

CHAPTER NINE

A QUESTION OF RIGHTS AND ETHICS

There is another side to becoming a successful writer...the BUSINESS of writing. It's fine to mail your masterpiece, have it accepted first time out, feel the surge that happens when you see your name in print and get paid for it!

It goes beyond that moment of elation. The following chapters are intended to give you a working knowledge of all facets of the writing life.

You really do have to consider such mundane things as copyright and libel suits. You need to know if you are working for 72 cents an hour. You also need to know how to communicate with the tax department.

Let's start with one of the most fundamental issues.

COPYRIGHT

Copyright is the exclusive right to publish, reproduce or perform a work. Anything written by writers, whether poem, article, story or play, is referred to as literary work.

It is important because, without copyright, you have no control over the use of your work. Anyone can take what you have written and use it as their own without payment to you. Copyright enables you to sell your work, to expect income from it, and to protect the integrity of that work.

The freelance writer owns copyright the minute the words are on the paper unless it has been assigned to someone else. There are some exceptions, but you should avoid giving up copyright.

In the case of work being done under a contract of service, your employer owns copyright unless an agreement, denoting otherwise, has been reached. For example, staff writers on newspapers and magazines do not normally hold copyright to their work. Freelance writers do, however, unless stated differently.

Copyright can be registered with the Copyright Office of the federal government. Registration establishes ownership, without further proof, in the event of legal proceedings. This is not as clear-cut as it appears.

When a writer registers a manuscript, no details are listed. Copyright states only the title and that it is a literary work. If there is concern for the claim of ownership of any part of the work, you need to prove you wrote the contents.

The easiest way to do this is to mail yourself a complete copy of the manuscript, registered mail, and keep the envelope sealed. This method provides proof that you wrote the article before the postmarked date.

To obtain copyright without formal registration, you don't need to do anything. It exists automatically as soon as words are created. The work must be in material form, whether handwritten, computer disk, print-out, or tape recorded. You cannot copyright an idea.

There is a high degree of ethics between writers and publishers. Don't assume that a magazine stole your idea just because you see a similar story in print. Many people can, and do, have the same idea at the same time.

Canadian law does not demand that you indicate copyright on your work. However, in other countries, including the United States, a copyright symbol (a c in a circle), your name and the year of publication, must appear on the work. If you are sending out an unpublished manuscript, it is wise to include this information, minus the year, as it has not yet been published. Indicate the date of completion somewhere else on your manuscript.

By retaining copyright, you never lose ownership of your material. You give a publisher license to use it one time only.

Subsequent printing must be with your permission and further payment is required.

In all countries that have signed the Berne Convention, copyright lasts for the lifetime of the author plus 50 years. On death, it passes to the heirs so it should be dealt with in your will.

Caution must be exercised when dealing with other countries. Most western countries are signatories of the copyright convention and editors in the United States and many places in Europe follow the rules.

But, there are some who feel no guilt in ignoring them.

Laws are only as useful as your access to their protection. You may find it impossible to police your work abroad. The only safeguard you have is your relationship with the publisher.

COPYRIGHT BELONGING TO OTHERS.

Occasionally, we want to use the work of others in our own assignments. I mentioned seeking permission earlier in the book. Briefly, contact the publisher and ask that the letter be passed on to the holder of copyright if you want to quote more than a few words. If there is any doubt about how much you are using, ask permission.

There is an expression, "fair dealing", that says there is no infringement of copyright in the use of work for research, home study, review, or criticism.

If you reproduce a considerable amount of any published work, whether it be literary or lines from a song, you have infringed the author's copyright, unless it is fair dealing.

Plagiarism goes beyond infringement of copyright. It is the deliberate reproduction of another's work to pass off as your own, or the failure to acknowledge someone else's authorship when you have incorporated it into your manuscript.

Occasionally, you are unable to find the copyright holder. If a book has been out of print for several years, or if copyright has passed to heirs and you have made all possible effort to find them and cannot, you are still not free to use the material. You must apply to the Copyright Board (check your federal listings) for a license. In Canada, the address is: 56 Sparks St., Suite 800, Ottawa, Ontario. K1A 0C9.

If the writer died more than 50 years ago, you can use the work providing you acknowledge the source. If the work was first published after the author's death, the 50 year rule is from the date of publication. The estate can seek damages for infringement during this time.

There is also a question of moral rights. Moral rights are retained even when you have assigned your copyright for use. They are your claim to authorship, and the right to prevent any modification which puts your reputation in jeopardy.

Use of an unpublished work, such as a journal, breach moral rights as well as infringing copyright. Diaries, letters, tapes—anything produced in material form, is protected under the same 50 year copyright law, published or not.

If you try to use a published work by only slightly changing the form, you may be accused of plagiarism. It is permissable to use material for research and put the ideas in your own words.

REPROGRAPHIC RIGHTS

These rights deal with photocopies. Until recently, a writer had no way of knowing if his work was being used by teachers or organizations.

In Canada and the United States, these concerns are being addressed by assigning authority to representatives from writers' organizations. Signed licenses with school boards and governments that pay a yearly fee, give them the right to copy most materials. The monies collected are divided between the holders of copyright.

The new Copyright Act allows a collective to monitor photocopying, collect fees, and distribute money to the rightsholder.

LICENSING RIGHTS TO THE PUBLISHER

There are several categories of rights—all of which are confusing to a novice writer. Make sure you understand what each means and know what rights you are granting.

1. FIRST RIGHTS: This can mean first North American Rights, first English Language rights, First Canadian Rights...be sure you make it clear which license you are giving. All of them mean "one time right" of printing but to different markets.

If you gave First Canadian Rights then, technically, you can sell the same piece under First American Rights to the United States. However, the usual practice is to grant First North American Rights because of the overlap in the USA and Canadian markets.

Other first rights, such as English Language and French Language, are often sold separately because the markets they target are different. The same principle applies to North American, British, Australian, etc. first rights.

2. Second Rights gives the publisher the use of your work for a second printing without payment to you, or with remuneration you have agreed upon beforehand.

3. Reprint Rights tells the editor the work you have submitted has been previously published. It's a good idea to tell him where and when. Payment is less for reprint rights, but you are getting "money for old rope".

4. One Time Rights usually means the same thing as reprint rights. It is a way of saying that you are giving rights for one printing only, without telling the publisher where it was done before.

The writer normally licenses first North American serial rights. Serial identifies magazine or periodical rights as opposed to book rights.

You have marked your cover page with the rights you are granting but be sure the invoice, or contract with the publisher, also specifies those rights. Be aware that some publishers mark the rights on the back of their cheque to you. If this is the case, your endorsement is also a contract.

You may sell second or reprint rights as often as you can find a market. One word of caution—never sell competing markets the same material at the same time!

Submit your manuscript with a covering letter that tells the editor where and when the article was first published and include the rights you are now offering (reprint rights or one time rights). You can expect approximately 50% of the original payment.

Rewriting the same story, two different ways, and submitting it as "first rights" is more a matter of ethics than copyright law.

I have done this with success BUT I always wait a considerable length of time before placing the material. The focus is completely changed and I never hit competing markets.

This is possible with material from lengthy interviews. There are usually several subjects and points of view that can be reworked.

The article that has made me the most money is one covering a couple's 25th wedding anniversary. It was initially done as a reaffirmation of vows for a seniors magazine; then, as an Encounter Weekend programme for their newsletter; as a resort's wedding/honeymoon package, for a travel magazine; as the vows they wrote, for a bridal market; as the difference it made in the family, for a woman's magazine...and I'm still selling it. All were sold as first rights because the material and the market was entirely different.

You know what rights you are prepared to license but the editor has a different idea. He wants additional rights. Now what do you do?

You must weigh this carefully. There are publications that buy only All Rights. If you are going to make the sale, you must comply.

Editors don't usually do this so they can resell your work. They like their publications to be exclusive. The last thing they want is to see the same article come out in a similar publication soon after, or worse, before, they have printed it.

If you're sure you'll have no further use for the material, then selling all rights may be worthwhile because most publishers pay higher for the exclusivity. But, be sure this is what you want to do.

A writer friend of mine, breaking into the market, was offered $2,000.00 for all rights to a short story. She was elated—this was big money! She signed without question and, for years, has been watching that story on television with no compensation to her except seeing her name: from a short story by....

It's rare, but there are editors who reprint material without the author's consent and without additional remuneration. It's the responsibility of the writer to stop him from continuing this practice.

If he claims ignorance, then he should be willing to pay the difference. If the practice continues, then report the publication to your professional group. Other writers must be warned and action taken. This is the only way we have of controlling the conduct.

Electronic reproduction into a database is a growing problem. I had no idea that some of my work was included until I was given a catalogue of available resource material. Three of my articles were there, for anyone to use, with no compensation to me. Now I state on my manuscript and in the covering letter that the material is not available for use in database without further negotiation.

This also applies to articles sold to newspapers. To ensure that the publisher cannot send your material to a wire service, write on your manuscript: syndication rights to be negotiated separately.

Rights are for your protection. Know what you're granting and be prepared to lose a sale if the demand is too high. There are other markets.

LIBEL CHILL

Libel is a printed statement, or photograph, that exposes an individual to hatred, contempt or ridicule; that implies immorality, criminal action, or disorderly conduct; that injures the professional reputation of the person; or touches on anything that might discredit him. This can apply to corporations as well as individuals.

If you make such statements, you are automatically in a position to be sued.

In Canada and Britain, the person who claims to have been libelled, needs only to prove the statement was published and you, as the author, must prove no libel took place. The presumption is against the author.

In the United States, the onus lies with the petitioner to prove that the writer and/or the publisher intended malice. The presumption is not against the author.

As a writer, you must do your best not to make unfair or inaccurate reference to any living person. Libel suits are complex and expensive. Even if you succeed in your defense, the costs of the court case are seldom reimbursed. These costs, at best, will be in the order of $10,000.00.

Publishers carry libel insurance that is not available to individual writers. To add to the situation, more and more publishers are asking their writers to sign contracts that state the author of the work has the responsibility of proof.

If the publisher is sued, along with you, you can be asked to cover any settlements and costs incurred by the publisher.

There are signals to look for in your work. The first is using the word systematically. For example: EVERY act the mayor did was calculated to improve his position. He SYSTEMATICALLY misled council.

If there is a pattern that you wish to expose, you must show it—not tell it. This can be done by using a list of proven examples. Saying he did it every time will cause you to lose your defense because a lawyer can prove that, one time, somewhere, he didn't do it.

Second, be extremely careful with criminal conduct charges. This is an easy law suit and all the subject has to do is prove you published it. To make such charges, you must have witnesses who are willing to go to court. You need hard evidence, no hearsay, and no conclusions.

If you accuse someone of criminal conduct, you'd better be able to prove it because the burden of proof is on you. The other side of this is when a court has found the person guilty. You can write all you want—the words are no longer accusations.

The third signal is when something "sticks out like a sore thumb". You've read through your article and everything follows the focus of the story. All of a sudden, one sentence doesn't fit. You've said something along the lines of: he was known to be involved with drugs in the 1960s. The article is on refinishing furniture.

The person sues and he's going to win. There was no reason, other than malice, for you to include this information. It is damaging and it isn't relevant.

Don't buy into the premise that the use of fictitious names, or a statement saying, that any resemblance between people living or dead is purely coincidental, will protect you from the possibility of a libel suit. If the reader associates a person with one described in your article, and the description reflects badly on that person's reputation, there is a danger of libel.

Publications are conscientious when it comes to libel because the publisher must be prepared to defend the truth of the statement, privilege, and fair comment.

These three things—truth, privilege, and fair comment— are your only means of defense. Let's have a look at each one in turn.

If the author's statements are true and accurate, and can be proven without doubt, then there is no basis for action for libel. If taken to court and you have hard proof, you will win.

Privileged reports can be either absolute privilege or qualified privilege.

Absolute Privilege occurs when a fair and accurate report, without editorial comment, on proceedings heard before a court of justice, is published at the same time they took place.

Qualified (conditional) privilege is enjoyed by reporters covering proceedings in any government body, whether legislative, administrative, a commission of inquiry, or any organization whose members represent the public. It doesn't matter if what you write is true or not—you are not stating opinion, you are relating what has been done or said.

Fair and honest comment on matters of public interest, as long as it's accurate and true, is privileged. Fair comment extends to criticism of books, magazines, articles, plays and films, and to the writing of a biography.

The author of any biographical piece is permitted to express honest opinion and give fair criticism of the works or accomplishments of the person, because it is of public interest and serves a useful purpose.

The only way libel suits can be won under laws of privilege is to prove "actual malice". This is the publication of false, defamatory material with the knowledge that it is false.

Proving that the writer and/or the publisher had a high degree of awareness, is difficult at best. The law weighs heavily in favour of the writer. However, if you are dealing with potentially dangerous editorial text, play it safe. Have the magazine clear the article with their legal representatives.

The easiest way to avoid a libel suit against you and/or the magazine is to refrain from using any statements that could be harmful in any way to another person.

INVASION OF PRIVACY

The arrival of the electronic age brought with it listening devices, closed circuit television, and the ability to eavesdrop on private telephone conversations.

Protection of privacy has become foremost in the minds of many. It is your responsibility, as a writer, to respect the privacy of others. Individuals are protected in the following ways:

1. From intrusion. A writer must not force himself into any situation where he would not reasonably be. For example, you cannot crash a private gathering, obtain damaging information, and use the material.

2. From the use of names or likeness, without permission, for the purpose of advertising or trade. There are cases where a celebrity look-alike is hired to endorse a product. The court will always rule in the favour of the celebrity who did not give permission.

3. From being falsely portrayed to the public. This invasion usually takes place when the writer is working with sensational material. For example: A statesman is reported to be in conflict of interest. Financial statements are disclosed that suggest he has made large profits from that conflict.

4. From publicly revealing embarrassing facts even if they are true. This occurs when a writer reports on an incident and

reveals extraneous material, such as colour, creed, or sexual orientation.

The question of protection of privacy comes back to your professionalism. The rule, if in doubt, don't, is a good one. More than one writer has been bankrupted by ongoing litigation.

CHAPTER TEN

RUNNING YOUR BUSINESS

Writing is your business. One of the reasons you are doing this is to make money. Every writer goes through that period of "working in the red" while establishing his career, but this is a condition neither you, nor the tax department wants to see continue.

You must have a "reasonable expectation of profit" otherwise your business will be viewed as a hobby. Right from the first day that you pick up a pen, start taking your manuscript records, and accounts payable and receivable, seriously.

You need to know where every article is, the dollar amount of your expenditures, and your earnings.

But, you are a writer not a bookkeeper, so you want to do this as quickly and easily as possible.

Everyone finds their own method, one that usually evolves with their career. The structure I am going to suggest is a simple way of starting. You make the modifications that suit your needs.

A card index is the first step in record keeping. I have 3" x 5" lined cards, one for the manuscript name and one for the magazine's name.

The manuscript card tells me where the article is and the status. When it's accepted, I add the date of publication, the payment date and amount. This gives me immediate access to information needed when corresponding with the original publisher, or dates should I want to license reprint rights.

The publisher's card contains the name of the editor with whom I am working, the name of the manuscript and the date it was submitted, and any information on publishing, including payment.

A card, headed ACCOUNTS PAID and the year, lists by month those sales which have been completed. A second card, ACCOUNTS OUTSTANDING, lists the acceptance date and the date payment is to be made. We'll cover the various forms of payment, shortly.

I have computer backup files of these records but, because I spend most of my waking hours with word processing, I keep these for cross reference only. I don't want to exit my programme and access records each time an editor phones—or I start wondering about the status of a submission.

The card index takes up little room, is an instant reference, and encapsulates everything I need to know. The contracts, letters of intent, and assignments are in the filing cabinet. The file-folder is marked REVENUE. I now find it useful to have one for each year but, in the beginning, I kept only one folder.

Any publishing information, from the letters or contracts, is noted in the magazine's file and in the card index.

For tax purposes, I keep a ledger of monthly expenses and income. This gives me a good idea of what I am, or am not, making. The income tax department is good to writers but it insists that you prove everything! Further in the chapter, I will deal with tax records.

Think about the cost of your writing—stationery, postage, automobile expenses, video and audio tapes, photocopies, computer and fax machine supplies, telephone, office rent (even in your home), research material and permission fees.

True, in the beginning you will be subsidising your passion. As time goes on, and you see the gap between loss and profit closing, you will become more than slightly interested in the bottom line.

It is unrealistic to set, and request on submission, an hourly rate that includes research, travel and writing time. No editor is going to pay you that much! I begin with real costs and deduct that from the payment. If I'm really in a mood to punish myself, I divide the amount that's left by the hours I worked. Usually, it comes out below minimum wage and to concentrate on that is nonproductive.

Let's have a look at the whole picture.

ASSIGNMENT:

2500 word article @ 10 cents a word	$250.00
3 photographs @ $15.00 each	$ 45.00
Total	**$295.00**

EXPENSES:

Research time, 7 hours @ $10.00	$ 70.00
Fax and phone expenses	$ 13.50
Long distance interview phone	$ 21.80
Courier	$ 10.00
Stationery, etc	.$ 10.00
Total	**$125.30**

DIFFERENCE BETWEEN INCOME AND EXPENSES=$169.70

WRITING TIME = 12 hours

INCOME PER HOUR = 169.70 divided by 12 = $ 14.14

To bring up the rate per hour, you can cut your expenses or negotiate with the editor for an increase in payment.

Assuming the article has been accepted from a query letter, let's have a look at the expense sheet. If the editor insisted on a courier, then the costs should be picked up by him. If not, could the manuscript have been mailed or faxed?

What about research time? Could it have been less? Will you be able to use some of this research in other articles? If so, the profit will increase when you use it.

If a long distance phone interview is necessary, should this not be the responsibility of the editor? The same applies to charges from faxes he has requested.

Reasonably, your expenses could have been cut by more than half. As you become more experienced and are able to predict costs with greater accuracy, you will be in a position to negotiate with the editor. Most publications are willing to accept responsibility for many expenses if you are fair in your requests.

Renegotiating an agreement can be difficult so it's much better to cover everything the first time. And get it in writing.

If you find yourself in the position where expenses have surpassed your expectation, and you feel you cannot absorb the costs, then you have two options.

1. Write or phone the editor and tell him that you have accumulated unexpected expenses, or that you have had to invest far more time than anticipated. Tell him you require X number of dollars more to make the contract viable. He will either say yes or no.

2. If he says no, and you are confident you can sell your work elsewhere, then you can refuse the offer...but do it courteously. You never want to shut an editor's door.

If, however, you are uncertain about another market, then you'd be wise to back-track and accept the offer. By the time you send out query letters, mail the manuscript, and take a chance on getting a higher rate of pay, you will have lost whatever you gained. You could even end up selling it for less than the original offer.

If you decide to drop your request, you must do it with care. You don't want to give the editor the impression that you are a push-over for any price he offers. Be sure you have thought through all possible actions and reactions before you make the phone call or write the letter.

I stay with the deal I've made. If I misjudged my hours, then it's my loss. The only time I ever ask for expenses to be picked up, beyond that which was agreed upon, is if I find the editor unreasonable in his demands for additional work or service.

I'm sure it's obvious that renegotiation is the least desirable position. Think through your contract requirements before an agreement is reached.

Don't forget that it's often to your advantage to accept fair market value, even if your expenses are high, to acquire the credit for your portfolio. Do a good job, meet your deadline, and you could find yourself in a better bargaining position the next time you work for that editor.

PAYMENT FROM PUBLISHERS

There are two methods of payment: on acceptance and on publication.

Payment on acceptance means the publisher sends you a cheque as soon as he decides to use your work. If, for some reason, he ends up scrapping it, you are still paid in full.

Payment on publication means your cheque is held until after the article has been published. This can be immediately after, or as long as 60 days after, publication. If the editor decides not to use the work, then you may be paid a kill fee (partial payment) or you may have your work returned with no payment at all.

Obviously, the one with the most advantages is payment on acceptance. Magazines do go under. The editor could have been holding your material for a year or more, only to return it without compensation. Then, there is the question of holding an article so long the material is no longer relevant. Again, it is returned and you might get a kill fee...if you're lucky.

The practice of holding articles, for payment on publication, is becoming the rule rather than the exception. The publisher wants to build inventory, to draw from as there are spaces to fill. Slush piles, with the rewrites the manuscripts often require, are time consuming. An editor would rather do the preliminary work at his leisure, keep the material on hand, and pay you when it's used.

Like every other writer, I like to be paid when I am accepted. However, there is a way to make paying on publication work for you. If you can establish an ongoing relationship with an editor, and have them buy most of the articles you submit, you can insure predictable income for a long period of time.

One magazine I freelance for has articles for the next two years. They are stable, with a large readership, so I'm not concerned about them stopping publication. Get your manuscripts out because a few markets like this can put you in the enviable position of having a steady income.

I'm told, one of the pleasures of writing is the unpredictable nature of your finances. Often, a writer doesn't know exactly what he will be paid until the article is in print. That might be exciting when you open the mail but it's hard on the nerves. I try to know exactly what my income is going to be.

Magazines pay by word or by assigned piece. If you are working with a publication that pays per word, you know where you stand on completion of the article.

This method of payment is as varied as the publications. The range can be from 1/4 cent to $1.00 or more per word. Don't assume you know what the pay scale is from market source material or information gleaned from other writers. Ask the editor before an agreement is reached.

If you know you are working for 7 cents a word, and you have to make X number of dollars to cover your expenses, you can control income by the length of the article. Even if you are given a maximum word count, this can be accomplished by setting limits on your expenses.

Payment per assignment is a flat rate for the package, often including photographic submissions. Again, magazine rates vary. Never accept an assignment without knowing what the pay scale will be.

CONTRACTS

Contacts between writer and editor are often verbal. Misunderstandings do occur but they are rare. The practice of not using written contacts is one based on practical application. If written contacts were issued for every article purchased, the editor would have little time to do anything else. If an editor tells you he will pay a certain price for a story, you can trust him to do that.

I work with a few editors that do send brief, contractual letters, usually after the details have been worked out. Others send out contracts with payment, telling what rights they have licensed and the amount paid. For income tax purposes, both have a distinct advantage because of the record they supply.

However, most editors receive the material after having told me the pay scale and an approximate publishing date. A cheque arrives, along with copies of the magazine, and my endorsement becomes the contract.

In this case, you must be very careful to keep an accurate accounting. You cannot afford to forget that a publisher paid you...and it's easy to do. Immediately upon receipt of the monies, add it to your records files. The publisher tells the income tax department whom he paid, so you'd better tell them you got the cheque!

A publisher has the legal right to hold a manuscript for two years before either using or returning it. If this is unacceptable to you, grant him rights of publication for 1 year (not less, they often need that much time) and state that the submission will be withdrawn after that date.

If the article has come out in the magazine and you have not received payment shortly after the agreed time, phone the editor and politely ask if he has forgotten. He should tell you the date the cheque will be mailed.

Should you still not hear from him, then write a firm, but polite, letter. If this brings no response, a registered letter, containing an invoice, is the next step. If that fails, you will have to take him to the grievance committee of your professional organization. Editors don't like this because they are "red flagged" and freelance submissions stop. Usually, upon threat of grievance, payment is prompt. You may lose the market but, do you want it?

One of the other problems that can arise is receiving less than the amount agreed upon. It's usually a pittance, say $15.00 or failure to pay for all the photographs used, but if the editor continues this practice with all of his writers, he has saved a considerable amount of money.

The theory, I'm sure, is that the money is so small the freelancer won't bother to fight it. Well, this one does, if only as a matter of principle. I've done my best for him and I expect him to keep up his end of the bargain.

I don't even phone. I invoice for the balance, with a time limit on the date payable. If nothing happens, I contact my professional group and have them threaten grievance. I don't care if I lose the market.

Fortunately, these occurrences are few and far between. Over the years, I've had dealings with a great many editors and have only had problems with two of them—and, by choice, have not submitted to either one since.

A word about editors. They come with a variety of titles and you are expected to know where your work should be directed. Until you have a working relationship with a magazine, this can be confusing.

Usually, the masthead is fairly clear but it is to your advantage to know what each title means.

1. ACQUISITIONS EDITOR: He is primarily responsible for soliciting, evaluating, and purchasing manuscripts. Usually edits the manuscripts he has acquired.

2. ASSISTANT EDITOR: Also referred to as Associate Editor. He can be anything from a secretary to an acquisitions

editor. Often, this is the person who replies to your query letter—especially if it's a rejection.

3. CONSULTING EDITOR: Usually a freelance editor who has been hired by the publisher to offer opinion or expertise. If the project is technical, or in some way out of the publication's range of specialization, the Consulting Editor will stay on to oversee the manuscript.

4. CONTRIBUTING EDITOR: Someone who writes for the publication as well as acts as an editor. Occasionally, a writer of note may be given the honourary title, Contributing Editor, as a perk.

5. COPY EDITOR: He reads through the manuscript, word for word, making the changes and corrections required before the work goes to the printer.

6. DEPARTMENT EDITOR: Found in the larger publishing houses where editorial content is divided into sections, genre, or series. There will be one editor for each department.

7. EDITOR: A term that covers anyone involved with editing.

8. EDITOR-AT-LARGE: A staff editor who handles different tasks, depending on circumstances. He can also be a freelance editor or a consulting editor.

9. EDITOR-IN-CHIEF: The person in charge of the entire editing function.

10. ASSISTANT TO THE EDITOR: An editor's assistant. Duties range from secretary to editing.

11. EXECUTIVE EDITOR: Usually the senior editor, editor-in-chief, or managing editor.

12. FREELANCE EDITOR: Hired by the publisher as an independent working on a project-to-project basis.

13. MANAGING EDITOR: Oversees the operations of the publication. He is usually the editor-in-chief's right-hand man.

14. PUBLISHER: The person in charge of everything that happens at a publishing house. He is responsible for the editorial department.

There are other classifications in the editorial department but these are the ones you need to know. You want your manuscript read in the shortest possible time so direct it to the correct editor.

A good place to start is with the Department Editor (name from the masthead of the magazine). He might be a Features Editor, Travel Editor, Crafts Editor, and so on.

If there are no departments, then send it to the Managing Editor, the Editor, or the Assistant Editor. If you have had some previous correspondence with the magazine, direct your submission to that particular person.

THE TAX DEPARTMENT AND YOU

I can speak with some authority on this subject because, after a few years of fairly large tax refunds against other income, I was audited. This is a frightening position to be in so make sure you know what—and WHAT NOT—you are entitled to claim.

I advise you to get a copy of the tax act as it affects you. This can be done by calling the tax department or by going to the library. The following suggestions are taken from my own experiences and are not intended to be a tax guide.

Basically, writers fall into three classifications:

1. Employees on salary who supplement their income by earning extra money with freelance work.

2. Part-time writers who are working at another job only until they are able to make a living writing.

3. Full-time, self-employed writers who are not on any payroll.

Writers with other jobs need only to attach a statement of writing income and expense to their tax returns. Any profit must be added to taxable income. Losses may be used to reduce taxable income.

Full-time writers must keep far more detailed records.First of all save everything! I have an accordion file that contains nothing except those receipts which will be submitted at the end of the year.

When I buy anything that has to do with writing or the office, I come home and drop the slip in the file. I don't carry it around for days and I don't put it on my desk to get lost in the paper war.

The income tax department treats writers generously. You are entitled to claim all your equipment, office rent and furnishings, supplies, paper, postage, couriers, long distance phone calls, travel relating to your work, business entertainment, automobile, professional membership dues, lawyer and accounting fees, reference books, copyright and permission charges, photocopying...in short, anything that relates to income.

If you are renting an office away from your home then the deduction is straightforward. The rent is claimed as an expense. However, if the office is a room in your house, you must be accurate.

Measure the floor space that you use exclusively for your work. In my case, it is 15% of the total floor space in the house. This 15% is the base for all other expenses that are incurred in running the business.

This rent is a deductible expense but, in Canada, it cannot be written off against other income to increase a loss. On the other hand, it can be carried forward for several years to be used as profits increase.

Power, heat, garbage, insurance, taxes, minor repairs and ordinary maintenance are all listed as 15% of the total yearly expense. For example. If my heating bill is $1286.00 for the year, my office expense is $192.90.

The only exception to this is the telephone expenses. If you have an extension of the main phone in your office, you are only entitled to the cost of long distance calls, the argument being that you would have the phone even if you weren't writing, but you wouldn't be making the long distance calls.

A separate line into your office, including a fax line, allows you to deduct all of the expense. Study the figures and see if this second line is worth your while. I have an extension of the main phone on my desk and a separate line for the fax phone (which can be used as voice) on the computer table. I claim all of the fax line, and the long distance calls on the main line.

Automobile deduction can be handled in two ways. If you have your car insured for business, then you are entitled to the full deduction of all those expenses relating to your writing. This includes repairs and insurance, as well as gas and oil.

If you have your car insured as pleasure only, then you are entitled to a deduction of X number of hours per month. The time allotted depends on your policy. Check with your insurance company to find out how much you are allowed for business.

Weigh these figures carefully. The cost of business insurance is higher and may not offset the amount you deducted. You might be better off to take the cheaper rate (pleasure only) and claim the maximum allowed under that policy.

No matter which you choose, careful records must be kept. A notebook, for recording milage, should be in the car at all times. If you go to the post office and you drive 1.6K, then record the time, date, and distance. Get into the habit of doing this! An auditor will insist upon seeing a log.

Gas receipts, repair bills, insurance costs, when insured for pleasure only, are handled on a percentage basis. If you are allowed to drive 4 hours a month you may claim 5.4% of the total of all automobile expenses.

File all income honestly. Publishers do not usually issue income slips so you are on the honour system. They do, however, declare you as an expense and in this day of computer technology, it is difficult for you to hide.

By the very nature of their work, writers are often subjected to audit. It is nothing to be fearful of if you have been honest and have kept good records. I mentioned the journal I keep as a monthly accounting of income and expenses. At the end of the year, I do all the totals, attach adding machine tapes and submit it, along with all my receipts (grouped by category of expense—office, postage, travel—in separate envelopes) to my accountant.

The bill is minimal because all he has to do is complete and submit the tax return. If I have done something terribly wrong, he keeps me out of the glue.

Accountants are well worth the money because tax laws change. Every country, province or state has their own set of taxes and rules. You will find yourself using accounting services more as your business grows, so pick a firm you like and get to know them.

Treat the business of writing like any other business and you 'll be on the right track.

CHAPTER ELEVEN

MARKET INFORMATION

While it is a good idea to start with subjects you know, eventually your creativity will force you to explore the unknown. Good research and your technical skill will allow you to write for any market that sparks your interest.

Some of the most fascinating assignments are those that teach you something. It's impossible to delve into the unfamiliar without discovering new and wonderful things, all of which you'll use later. Recently, I was at a meeting of my professional group when one of the members asked me about something I was working on. It happened to be an article about cats.

He inquired if this was a good market and I assured him it was. The next question was about my cat. When I told him I didn't have one, the shocked reply was something along the lines of, how dare you write about cats when you own a dog!

It's easy. I know what a cat is. I like them. There is an abundance of research material. I also write for a religious magazine that is not of my faith (and one that is), for the retirement market when I'm working, for a parenting magazine after my children are grown, for travel markets when I never get far enough away from this computer to travel. You get the idea.

With a little experience, you can write about anything.

The following list of markets is to give you an overview of what's out there. Researching your target market is something you have to do for yourself.

ANIMALS
This market is open to the beginning writer. These magazines are aimed at everything from the pet owner to the professional breeder. They are specific to the animal—cats,

dogs, horses, etc. They usually pay per word and the scale is advertised in market sources and guidelines. Submissions normally require photography. Good transparencies can make the cover.

ARTS

Some expertise is required to write for publications covering the arts. They range from literary and visual, to criticism and review. The best chance for a freelance writer trying to enter this market, is to profile an artist. National arts magazines are difficult to break into but the pay scale is high. Local publications are easier, and the pay scale reflects this.

The editor will want to see photographs of the artist and/or the work.

BUSINESS

Business writing can be divided into two categories, writing for the layman and writing for the business community. Articles done for the average person take business jargon and information, place it in language that is easily understood, and present it in an interesting way.

Articles written for the "in crowd" provide the kind of detail the businessman will find useful in the daily operation of his enterprise, in making wise investment choices, or in planning for the future.

The business writer has a great deal of freedom to interject opinion with facts. A background in economics, accounting, or some form of management, is important because you are writing as an authority. You must be able to find your way around the business community, be accepted by them, and have a working knowledge of the language.

A feature can be written about any item or industry that makes a living for it's inventor, organizer or distributor. Don't be afraid to approach the executive for an interview. It's free advertising for him so he will most likely be happy to supply you with all the information you need.

The success of your article will depend on your ability to inform and inspire, whether you are writing for the layman or the businessman.

CHILDREN

The nonfiction children's market is a growing one. These days of computers and interactive television have made CHICKEN LITTLE tiresome to the young reader.

Don't assume it's easy writing for kids—it's not! This is one of the most difficult markets. Not only must you have the ability to tap into their point of view, but you must keep up with their language. This is not to say you use their slang—it would be out of fashion before the article got into print—but it is imperative that you know how to communicate with them. Humour is often the way to a young reader's heart.

There is a special kind of writing for each age group and the only way to find out what that is, is to read a number of magazines before you start.

Children look for facts and information in the articles they read, just as adults do. Never talk down to them. Learn to tell them about the things that concern them and do it at a level they can understand.

EXPOSÉ

Exposé articles are always in demand. The advancement in our technology has produced many ingenious methods of perpetrating crimes and exploiting victims. This leaves you with a readership that insists on the truth.

As a writer, you are in the position of offering help and protection from these injustices. When you produce verified exposés, you serve society by improving their quality of life.

The best way to break into this market is to keep a file of all reports covering fraud, conflicts of interest, scandals—generally, those violations that cause you to seethe with indignation. Know what's out there and then start tracking the truth.

When writing the article, you must be careful to give the other side of the story. Just because one person or organization is unethical, it doesn't mean that everyone in the same field follows the same practice.

The threat of libel is high. Go over your work carefully and look for the signals that were outlined in the section on libel. There must be evidence that wrongdoing exists.

Painstaking research is essential. Every fact must be verifiable and all information up-to-date. When you write your article, involve your reader so that he sees how the offence affects him.

At the end of your article, suggest remedies with examples of why/how they could work. Whether these remedies are many or few, they must be beneficial enough to make your exposé a service to the public. It must be a complete article..."What can be done about it?", not simply, "What's wrong?".... to help society.

A point of interest. You can write an exposé article about a person who is deceased without fear of libel, providing you do not involve living heirs.

FAMILY
This market is one of the better ones for the writer trying to break in because it lends itself to personal experience stories.

Here, you'll be able to share those things which have influenced your child or your home, have made a difference in education or health, or have improved your daily living. The topics are as varied as the publications. Read several magazines, look for trends, and come up with an angle.

HEALTH AND FITNESS
Health and fitness is a growing market because of today's increased level of awareness. Be interested in general fitness, healthy foods, and exercise to be successful in this field. You are writing for a specific group of people, often

dedicated, and they will spot you a mile away if you don't believe what you are saying.

This market covers things like low fat, salt-free cooking, new medical findings, the latest exercise equipment. It is necessary to keep an eye on what has been published and what trends are surfacing.

HISTORY

All you need to be successful in this market is the ability to make history come alive. The interest in folklore increases with people's struggle to return to their roots.

One of the most important things to remember is that you must tie the past in with the present. You need to show your reader what it is about "yesterday" that influences "today".

Your material will only be as interesting as the people who made things happen or had things happen to them. It is imperative that you build human interest into your characters and incorporate drama into the events. For example, it would be unwise to write a history of the Gulf War without focusing on one of its heros. Sift through the facts until you find the angle that is going to make this a real-life experience for your reader.

Study the media and see if you can find a link between your historical piece and today's news. History is told and retold, from many points of view. It is up to you to find the hook that will capture an editor's attention and a reader's imagination.

This market can include everything from stories about your grandparents to in depth studies of world events. The range is wide. Take advantage of it. The use of old photographs, maps, and documents give weight to your submission.

HOBBIES AND LEISURE

A market tailor-made for the freelance writer! When it comes to hobbies, everyone is an expert. We all know the best way to fill our leisure hours.

There are magazines out there for every type of craft and all are looking for a new idea, an original pattern, a helpful hint. There are magazines for every imaginable recreation, at all levels of income and expertise.

Have a look through the newsstand, pick out a few publications that focus on your areas of interest, study their editorial policy, and start writing. Support photography will likely be requested.

HOME & GARDEN

The most important thing to remember when writing for this market is that your reader doesn't want to know what you did with your home or garden...he wants to know what to do with his.

If you only have success growing weeds, and turn the bulbs backwards in the light sockets when changing them, read these articles—don't write them.

But, if you have a yard boasting laden kiwi vines, or have taken a "fixer-upper" and turned it into a mansion, then this is a lucrative market for you.

Tell the reader what he can do to accomplish what you did. Tell him step by step how easy it is. Write an article filled with tips and encouragement.

The editor will likely request photographs and scale drawings, so be sure you tell him, when you query, what you can supply.

HOW-TO

This is not an article that can be done successfully by research alone. If you don't know how-to, then you can't possibly be effective in telling someone else how-to.

Whatever the focus, the article will be heavy with hands-on experience. Don't ever try to write directions for a reader without first following them yourself. All technical terms must be defined.

The temptation to "preach" to your reader is strong. Try to keep your opinions out of your writing unless they serve some useful purpose.

How-to articles fall into three basic categories: the practical how-to, the philosophical how-to, and the psychological how-to. Briefly, they are as follows:

1. Practical. These are the how-to build, how-to fix, how-to make, features. They are instructional and complete with detailed drawings, blueprints and photographs.

They also include the self-help how-tos. How to lose weight and keep it off, how to manage your money, how to be successful with your exercise programme.

The article is written with a clear, no-nonsense approach because you speak with authority. After all, you are telling your reader how to change a physical part of his life that is making him uncomfortable.

2. Philosophical. The subjects covered in these articles pertain to moral and spiritual values. These include, the benefits of positive thinking, how to gain peace of mind, how to increase your creativity by using the power of your mind. They are mystical issues with a practical application.

The markets for these articles are usually found in religious publications. The most effective approach is to use example and anecdote rather than straight narrative that runs the danger of dissolving into "preaching".

3. Psychological. The line is fine between the psychological how-to and the philosophical how-to. While the latter finds its strength in the mystical, the psychological how-to is concerned with the intellect.

It is mental reconditioning—how to find love, how to be popular, how to achieve happiness. They are positive suggestions for conquering negative habits, (worry, jealousy, fear, anger, addictions).

It can either be written as "How you can", "How I did", or "How he did". Each has its own place and the one you use will be in keeping with the focus of your story and the editorial policy of the publication.

In writing these articles, your purpose must be immediately shown, either in the title or the introductory paragraph. It is your job to convince the reader that he needs to learn what you have to teach.

The directions must be logical, the style direct, and the instructions accurate.

HUMOUR

This is one of those, either you have it or you don't, situations. To a few, writing humour comes easily. To the majority, it is the most difficult assignment of all.

Unless you are naturally funny, don't try to write humour. Not only will you succeed in being less than amusing, you run the risk of sounding ludicrous and artificial.

LITERARY/ESSAY

These are notoriously low paying markets. They are listed as "little" markets for good reason, but there is compensation for the lack of remuneration—prestige.

Almost without exception, the essays are literary works, heavy with intellectual opinion, and there are as many subjects as there are points of view. Often, the opinion or living page of your local newspaper is a good freelance market, and literary magazines, often published by universities, welcome submissions.

MEN'S

High-paying men's magazines want male orientated topics discussed by men for men. They are open to everything from self-help to humour, but all the articles are powerfully written. The best way to break into this market is by interviewing a personality of interest to the readership.

It is imperative that you read several issues of the publication you wish to query. Each has its own policy and format, and each focuses on a variety of subjects.

NATURE/ECOLOGY

This market is wide open. The reader is interested in what can be done, what he can do, and what the government is/is not doing to improve the environment.

The topics are varied—attracting song birds to your garden, saving the old-growth forests, keeping our water clean, preserving wildlife. Recycle, restore and re-use!

Publications are open to opinion articles, well researched instructional articles, interviews with everyone from officials to protesters, wildlife profiles, photographic features, news items.

Many of these articles border on expose, (industries that dump toxic waste), others are how-to, (how you can start a recycling programme in your neighbourhood), and still others are warm features on wildlife, (the nesting habits of water fowl).

In most cases photography is required. And be sure you can verify your information.

OPINION

Every newspaper has an opinion section open to the freelance writer. Unless you are accepted by a major national publication, you won't be paid well but it's a good place to gain some credits and tear sheets because established writers don't seek this market.

Well-written pieces are welcomed as long as they do not slander or defame, and are not used as a soap-box for any fanatical view.

Several magazines on the market also have sections open to freelance opinion. They are usually found in the first or last pages of the publication. Headings such as, The Last Word Is Yours or Small Talk, signal the use of this material.

The most successful subjects are those which address today's issues. Be fair, be factual, and be interesting.

PERSONAL EXPERIENCE

Personal experience articles can be written for any market. Everything that has happened to you, any time in your life, can be turned into income.

Tell your story with skill, empathy, and honesty. Tell your reader about obstacles you have overcome, about a difficult situation you have turned into an advantage or about a learning experience that could benefit them. Relate a humorous event from the past. Anything. If it's happened to you, it has, or will have, happened to someone else. There is always an interested reader.

RELIGIOUS

Writing for these publications can be lucrative. They survive because of well-written, freelance articles that are neither sanctimonious nor saccharine. You need an angle with a timeless message and a writing style that lets the reader identify.

You do not have to be of the denomination to write for the publication—faith is faith. You must be sincere and you must have something to say about a way to solve everyday problems.

Family dilemmas with practical solutions, how faith gave you the strength to overcome an adversity, the part God plays in your life, are all topics that will catch an editor's eye.

RETIREMENT

The abundance of magazines and news-letters, make this a perfect personal experience, survey, and information market. With the exception of a few up-scale publications, they welcome freelance material.

The easiest way to break into this market is to write a humorous, first person experience, a travel piece (unless the publication has a staff writer) or an exposé article that will benefit the retired.

Study the newspaper for financial updates, the latest scam, the newest medical breakthroughs—anything that can be turned into an interesting article.

SURVEY

Survey articles are as easy to sell as they are to write. It is possible to glean information, from news items and television, to build a feature. For example: famous people who have something in common.

You could cover, THE SUCCESSFUL WRITERS WHO HAVE HAD FIRST WORKS REJECTED or HOW DIVORCE BANKRUPTS THE HOLLYWOOD SET, simply by reading news releases.

Ideas for survey articles can come from everywhere. There are the familiar holidays and anniversaries. What about collecting opinions from well-known people, even the ones in your area for a local publication? You can rewrite a subject already covered if you change the angle and add your own unique style.

The ideas come from living with, and talking to, people.

TRADE PAPERS

Any trade, of any standing, has its own publication. BUILDING MONTHLY, POWER SMART, PLUMBERS NEWSLETTER, DATA COMMUNICATION, are examples of the kinds of titles that signal trade papers.

There are hundreds of these papers and they are one of the easiest markets to enter. The remuneration is modest but you can built a reasonable, steady income if you are submitting to several on a regular basis.

They want news of any kind that is connected with their trade: profiles of involved persons, schemes, new branches opening up, changes in staff, and internal news such as weddings, birthdays, deaths, etc.

Many useful items can be picked up from your local paper and rewritten to fit the format of the trade paper. Once known to the publisher, you will likely be called and fed information for the paragraph or two the editors require.

One word of caution. Don't submit to two papers covering the same trade. If you do, you'll soon be submitting to neither.

TRAVEL

The major publications have travel writers on staff, but this is still a market worth pursuing. For those publications accepting freelance work, there is a strong demand.

These articles have wide appeal. They help the person who travels organize their business or pleasure trips. They also bring enjoyment to the person whose only contact with other parts of the world is through the written word.

There are a few traps which novice writers tend to fall into...watch for them. Don't generalize. Instead of covering every one of the Hawaiian Islands, focus on one—then on a specific area of that island.

Don't paint a glowing picture. Point out the bad with the good. This gives your reader a realistic view. There is nothing worse than arriving at a destination and finding it far below your expectation. If your reader is an arm-chair traveller, he deserves to know what the area is really like. This is a learning experience for him as well as entertainment. Be truthful, but be fair.

The best thing about travel writing is that publications never seem to get too much of one place. Scenes change. Hotel and restaurants open and close.

To do the story properly, you have to travel to the place you're covering. Many airlines, hotels, restaurants, chambers of commerce, and tourist bureaus go out of their way to welcome travel writers. Once you make a name for yourself, you will pay very little to see some of the best places in the world.

Start building credits. Write about what you know for your local paper—perhaps a place you visited on your vacation. For national publications, write about those things in your home town that attract tourists. They might be commonplace to you, but they are exotic to someone else.

When you've amassed enough credits and tear sheets to give credibility, send out queries. Try to suggest assignments that aren't going to cost the publisher an arm and a leg. That way, you have a better chance of being accepted.

With a few assignments to your credit, you can set your sights higher...and higher....until you are travelling first class, all over the world, and getting paid for it!

WOMEN'S

Traditionally, women's markets have focused on beauty tips, health and fitness, romance, and domestic interests.

It is imperative that you keep up with every new magazine to hit the market because these are the ones which will buy your work. The larger the publication, the harder it is for a freelance writer to break in. Big houses are, for the most part, staff written and what freelance work they do accept is from established writers.

Submit recipes, survey articles, and opinion pieces on everything from sex to sewing. Challenge traditional views and offer advice to those who seek change in their lives. Share how-to, and how I did, articles and personal experience stories.

As credits increase and you have good tear sheets to submit with queries, the quality of the publication that accepts your work will increase as well. This is one of the highest paid magazine markets.

PHOTOJOURNALISM

The field of photojournalism deserves special note. Having its start after World War II, when correspondents began carrying their cameras out of necessity, it came into its own through magazines like LIFE and LOOK.

As a rule, photojournalists are not photographers but writers who carry cameras. When that award winning picture is published, it's usually one that happened by accident rather than by design.

Magazines lead the field in the purchase of these articles because most newspapers have staff writers and photographers who work together on assignments.

It is cheaper for magazines to pay for a "package" than it is to hire separately. Using freelance photojournalists has kept more than one publication in a profit situation.

As far as you're concerned, you'll earn more money by learning how to put together a proposal that includes photography. Should you try this? Of course. For several reasons.

1. You'll get more assignments.

2. You'll sell more articles that you submit on speculation.

3. You'll be paid more.

4. Your skills of observation will improve.

You don't need all that heavy, expensive equipment that professional photographers lug around. The following list will see you through most assignments.

1. Two, lightweight 35-mm, single lens camera bodies, one for black and white film and one for colour slides.

2. Four lenses. 28-mm wide angle, 35/85-mm zoom 100-mm telephoto and 200-mm telephoto. The 28-mm is wide angle and lets you shoot crowds and panoramic scenes. The

35/85-mm is a zoom lens with the ability to go immediately from wide angle to short telephoto. The 100-mm telephoto is used for portrait work and sporting events and the 200-mm lens is for long range shots such as yacht races.

3. Filters: yellow, red, skylight, and ultraviolet. These filters improve the quality of your pictures. Yellow and red will provide contrast between sky and clouds for black and white film, skylight reduces the blue cast that happens on some days, ultraviolet will cut glare and unwanted reflection. All filters protect the surfaces of the lenses from scratches.

4. A battery-operated flash, capable of taking night shots.

5. A light-weight, fabric carrying case that can be strapped around the waist. This is not a necessity as far as the photography goes but it lets you carry your equipment and write at the same time.

You will learn as you go. Develop your skills by reading many of the excellent books on the market. Subscribe to a magazine that covers your field of interest. Join a photography group. And practise, practise, practise!

If you have the resources, take a photography course. You will save yourself the costly mistakes of a trial and error process.

When you submit your query, tell the editor what photography is available. If the photos are crucial to your article, include a sample of your work.

It's best to send 8" X 10" black and white glossies rather than contact, or proof, sheets if you are submitting in film. The editor can really see the quality of your work. If you want to show him the variety available, you can include a contact sheet with the glossies.

Never include original slides in your submission. Copies cost very little. Send all slides in clear, plastic cases available from supply stores, identify each one, and mark them with the date and copyright sign.

Include a SASE for return of your photography. If the publisher insists on first and all rights, make him pay for them. You will never be able to use them again, once you sell the rights.

As your interest in photography increases, it will be to your advantage to build stock shots. You do this by taking rolls of film, print and slide, for inventory—an excellent "days-off" project.

When the need arises, you will be able go to your library of photographs, select those you need for submission, and save yourself a great deal of time and frustration. Nothing is worse than trying to get a photograph of spring flowers for an article with a November deadline!

CREATIVE NONFICTION

Creative nonfiction, or the "new journalism", came into being in the 1960s. Simply, it is the use of literary devices, formerly used exclusively in fiction, for writing nonfiction articles and reports.

It lends itself more to magazine writing than to newspaper reporting because the use of this method makes it impossible to keep the article short.

Study the work of Tom Wolfe, Truman Capote, Norman Mailer, and Terry Southern to familiarize yourself with this technique.

Personal Experience stories are the ideal entry into Creative Nonfiction. The subject lends itself to enhancement and you will likely be more comfortable beginning with something you know until you fully understand this form of expression.

BIOGRAPHY

The interest in biographies never seems to wane. Through other people's lives, we experience their problems, successes and failures, conflicts, actions and reactions.

All biographies offer the reader a rare glimpse into the personal and private lives of people they have admired, envied or emulated. If well-written, they offer a complete picture of that life and its meaning.

Strive for objectivity blended with subjectivity. Meld with your subject until you are one with his feelings, thoughts, dreams, defeats and victories.

The method of writing successful biographies follows a logical progression.

1. Choose a subject that is intriguing. If he doesn't interest you, he will not interest your reader. Check what has been previously written, study the angle used and come up with something different. If diaries, journals, letters, etc., are at your disposal you have a great advantage.

2. Review the articles and books that are on the market to find the current trend. Are the biographies focusing on minority groups? On famous women? On people who have made it in business?

Are they double featured: husband and wife, families, ethnic groups whose leaders have accomplished great things? Follow the trend, because you will sell, but look for the one thing that will make your work unique.

3. Painstaking research is a must. If your subject is living, or recently deceased, then interview everyone you can reach who was part of his life. Read all the letters, journals, etc., that are available to you.

Follow every avenue of research: archives, libraries, professional associations. Visit the places he lived and worked. Gather all possible facts regarding the life and times of your subject and verify every piece of information.

Keep in mind that research expenses, such as travel, tapes for interviews, fees for archives, etc., are all income tax deductible.

4. Select the material and prepare your outline. You will have far more in your notes and tapes than you can possibly use. Keep everything. Delete all information that detracts from the storyline or diffuses the character focus.

You must bring your character to life. Here, the phrase that drove me crazier than any other...show—don't tell...comes into play. Every editor that wrote me, in those beginning days, used these words and I had no idea how to fulfil the request!

The easiest way to do this in a biography, beyond the physical description, is to dramatize (show) your subject doing something. If there is an action, then there is "showing".

For example: Joe Smith ran down the road is telling you what Joe did.

Drenched in perspiration, Joe Smith tried to escape his pursuer is showing Joe running. It brings a vivid picture to your mind and heightens the interest.

Personality traits can also be dramatized. You can show gentleness, for example, by describing the way a large, gruff man interacts with a child.

He looked as if he could tear a phone book in half on the first try but, when he picked up the sleeping child, cradled her and carried her up the stairs, I was shocked to see tears glistening in his eyes.

5. The use of contrast is a valuable tool in writing biographies. This is evident in the preceding example. Contrast brings to life all facets of your subjects personality and physical traits.

By dramatizing successes and failures, short comings and perfection, temper and tolerance, the writer rounds out the character, making him real to the reader. Every interesting person has good and bad traits. Learn to recognize and use them.

6. No matter how many facets of personality you bring out, your subject will not be unique until you find the focal point that represents your attitude toward him.

Every person has something in his character that he projects above all others, and that is the trait you are looking for, whether it's sense of humour, anger, generosity, or ambition. Ask yourself, What is the single most important fact about this person? Pivot your story around it.

7. Every biography will have secondary characters and they must be as carefully researched as your subject.

These are the people who influenced him, who loved him and lived with him, the people who hated him. Anyone who came in contact with your subject is important.

Again, you will not use all your research but don't destroy anything. You may need to verify a fact or you may want to write a sequel.

8. Give your reader a sense of time. Recreate the surroundings in which your subject lived. Show the dress of the day, the social mores. Become as familiar with his world as you are with your own.

Biographies are a way for us to live history. They let the reader exist in other times. Anyone who wants to be part of Cook's travels or dance with Pavlova, can do so by picking up a book or a magazine article. You must recreate the time so vividly that your reader will become an eyewitness.

9. Write your article with style. Provide the key to understanding the subject and present it in such a way that it could be a movie.

You have followed an analytical progression: selected your subject, accumulated your research, made your outline, found the interesting twists. Now you must write the best article you can. Even though you are dealing with facts, it is your job to ensure that they are never dull.

AGENTS

The question of agents comes up from time to time. All new writers think how wonderful it would be if they could write, sit back, and let someone else sell their work.

Marketing is time consuming, expensive and frustrating. But, it is something you have to do for yourself. It is the only way you are going to learn what to write and for whom.

Agents don't want to sell magazine articles. Most pieces sell in the low hundreds of dollars—many below that. If an agent sells a piece for $100.00 and takes 15%, all he'll make is $15.00. It is unlikely his costs will be covered.

The other side of this is that magazine editors do not like dealing with agents unless they are purchasing book excerpts from a famous author's work. The minute they see an article submitted under an agent's letterhead, they start seeing big costs and lengthy negotiations. Usually, the rejection is automatic, no matter how good the manuscript.

THE FUTURE

Let's take a moment to look ahead. You are a success. All the things you have dreamed about and worked for are coming true.

You have been written up by your professional group and are attracting attention at a local level. The next step strikes fear in the heart of almost every writer I know. INTERVIEW AT A NATIONAL LEVEL!

Always assume this is going to happen. Then, when it does, you will be ready. Forget the fact that you've been living the solitary life. Put aside all those feelings of panic as soon as you're hit with more than 2 people, both of whom, love you.

Think about things like radio and television interviews. Live those days over and over in your mind before they happen. When they do, you can avoid everything from terror to frustration by pre-planning.

When the interviewer calls and asks for an appointment, find out what aspects of your life he wants to cover and what market he is representing.

If you have limits about what he can say, let him know. Refuse to answer everything that makes you uncomfortable but learn to do it in a way that isn't antagonistic. You may wish to prepare a list of questions you are willing to answer. Try to keep the them intriguing and to place a new angle on your work.

Anticipate his questions. A good way to do this is to interview yourself before the actual meeting. Go over your faults and failures as well as your strengths and successes. Look at your philosophy. Think about your attitude toward issues. Try to interject humour into your answers.

Recall the things you did when you were conducting an interview and reverse the situation. Instead of guiding the conversation, you are being guided.

Take your time with the answers. If you don't know, say so. Try and think about what your words will look like in print. Don't say more than you have to and be clear in all expressed opinions.

The interviewer should offer to let you see the article before it's printed. If he fails to do so, politely ask to read it, assuring him that it's to his advantage to let you do so. Tell him you understand the process of editing and that you know copy can be changed but content remains the same.

Never accept money or pay for an interview. This puts you in a position of debt to the interviewer and his publication.

Never lose sight of the fact that you worked very hard to get where you are. You have devoted your life to something you believe in. You have given a good part of your life to the obsession of writing.

Your interviewer should know you are proud of your work.

CHAPTER TWELVE

BITS AND PIECES

AWARDS AND GRANTS

I would like to tell you that financial help is available to you, the impoverished writer, but I can't. Most of what's out there goes to those already established.

The large, national grants are usually given to recognized authors during major writing projects, the aim being to support them while they complete a work in progress.

Nationally, there are some project and travel grants, and a few dollars are allocated to those "emerging" writers displaying promise, but the number of applicants are many and the dollars are few.

Regional grants are dependent on the resources of the individual governments. These, like the national grants, are routinely awarded to writers who have had some success.

Check the listings for government offices and talk to the people in charge of the arts programmes to see what's available to you.

An assortment of cash awards is given each year to honour those who have achieved writing excellence. The range of categories is broad, and many are available to the novice writer.

Other awards are bestowed, on the recommendation of professional associations, in recognition of published works. Many of these awards are international, particularly between Canada and the United States, and Canada and Britain.

Lists may be found in all the market source material, in newsletters, and writer's periodicals. Some are granted through competition—you pay an entry fee of a few dollars and your submission will be read and juried.

Enter as many as you can. Get your name out there. If you win, along with the cash comes recognition and a nice credit to add to your resumé. If you are not successful in taking one of the monetary prizes, all may not be lost. It's possible to catch the eye of an editor who will want to publish your work.

Right from the beginning of your writing career, keep a scrapbook. As your work is published, cut out and place one of the original articles (editors usually send you several copies) in your book. It's a good idea to keep a second scrapbook to house a photocopy. Of course, your file holds the copies to be sent out as tear sheets.

A scrapbook serves two purposes. It gives you instant access to what you have available for samples of your work. Look through the book, instead of sheet after mixed-up sheet of published copies, choose the ones you want to send with your submission, and then start going through the folder for the tear sheets.

Second, you can watch the progression of your work. The times when you're discouraged, you'll get a lift from looking back to see what you've accomplished. Reading back material can be an eye-opener! If, after 5 years, you still like the writing, you know you've done something really good! If you don't like it, chalk it up to professional growth.

I hope you've learned that writing is fun. It is a lifestyle all its own. Some days, you will be filled with despair...the "POOR MEs" will get you! Then, when you least expect it, something wonderful will happen.

It could be acceptance of a submission you were sure was lost. It could be a cheque coming just when the car insurance is due.

Best of all, it's seeing something you created, something belonging only to you, gracing the pages of a magazine.

It's a life you wouldn't give up for anything in the world.

GLOSSARY

ADVANCE. A sum of money a publisher pays to a writer prior to publication. In book publishing, the advance is paid against the royalties. (the money the book will earn). In major freelance work or work for hire, the advance is paid to help with research and/or travel expenses. It is partial payment of the contracted price; the balance due on completion.

ADVERTORIAL. Advertising copy written to represent an editorial feature. The work reads like an article but the word, advertisement, appears at the top of the page.

ALL RIGHTS. Giving up all rights and copyright to the publisher. The writer may not use the article again because it has become the property of the publisher.

ANTHOLOGY. A gathering of works by one writer, or a collection of works by several writers, published under one cover.

APOLOGY. The justification or defence of a writer's opinions or conduct. The apology does not usually imply blame as it does in the everyday sense of the word.

APOLOGIST. The defender of another person's beliefs, actions or work.

ARCHAISM. The use of words or phrases that are no longer commonly used in the language.

ASSIGNMENT. A specific piece, for an agreed price, that is requested by the publisher. The contracted amount is paid to the writer on completion of the work.

AVANT-GARDE. A body of writers who are dedicated to the idea of art as an experiment. They break from tradition in the effort to stay ahead of their time.

B&W. The abbreviation for black and white photographs.

BIBLIOGRAPHY. A list of writings by different authors, placed at the end of an article or book, that acknowledges the excerpts used by a writer when compiling research.

BIMONTHLY. Publications that are printed every two months.

BIONOTE. A brief paragraph about the writer that appears at the beginning or end of the article, or on the contributor's page.

BIWEEKLY. Publications that are printed every two weeks.

BUSINESS SIZE ENVELOPE. The standard sized envelope used in sending business correspondence. #10 envelope.

BYLINE. The author's name appearing with the published piece.

CAPTION. A description of the subject matter of a photograph.

CLEAN COPY. A manuscript free of errors, cross-outs, smudges and wrinkles.

CLIPPINGS. News items of interest to trade magazine editors. Those items clipped from periodicals that are filed for possible research.

CLIPS. Samples of the writer's published works. Also called tear sheets.

CLOSURE. The sense of completion at the end of a work. In literary criticism, the compression of a work's meanings to a single and complete sense that excludes the claims of other interpretations.

COMMISSIONED WORK. The editor assigns a specific article to the writer, to be paid for when the work is completed.

COMPATIBLE. The condition which allows one computer to share information with another computer.

CONNOTATION. A range of further associations that a word or phrase suggests in addition to the dictionary meaning. ie: describing a person as a "rat".

CONTRIBUTOR'S COPIES. Copies of the magazine, in which his work has appeared, sent free of change to the writer.

COPYEDITING. Editing a manuscript for spelling, punctuation and grammar, but not for subject content.

COPYRIGHT. The process which protects the writer's work from being reproduced without his permission.

COVER LETTER. A brief letter that accompanies the manuscript. This is not a query letter, but a letter that answers the editor's request for the manuscript.

CUTLINE. The words that identify the contents of a photograph. Also called a caption.

DESK-TOP PUBLISHING. A system of publishing that is designed for computers and has the capability of typesetting, layout, design, illustration and printing.

DISK. The round, flat metal plate on which computers store data.

DOT-MATRIX. A printed type that is composed of a pattern of tiny dots. The more dots, the better the print quality.

DOWNLOAD. To transmit programmes or data from a main computer to a smaller computer or terminal.

ELECTRONIC SUBMISSION. The submission of a query or manuscript by computer disk or modem.

ESSAY. A brief, written passage that discusses a subject or proposes an argument. It is less formal than an academic dissertation.

EXPOSITION. A systematic explanation of, or argument about, a subject.

FAIR USE. A provision in the copyright law that allows the use of short passages without infringing the owner's rights.

FAX. Abbreviation for facsimile. A machine that sends and receives printed messages over the telephone lines.

FEATURE. An article that gives the reader information other than news items. A term also used by magazines to identify a lead article or particular department.

FIGURE OF SPEECH. An expression that departs from the accepted literal sense, or the placing of words in contrast with one another for emphasis.

FILLER. A short item, such as an anecdote, verse, humour, or timeless news piece, used by the editor to "fill out" a magazine page.

FIRST NORTH AMERICAN SERIAL RIGHTS. The rights licenced by the editor to ensure first time publication, in North America, of the writer's work. These are the rights usually purchased by a periodical.

FIRST-PERSON NARRATIVE. A written work using "I" to tell the story. In nonfiction, the use of first-person is used for personal experience accounts or eye-witness reports.

FLESH IT OUT. An expression used by editors in criticism of a story. They are requesting that the writer expand the piece by adding more detail, description, or quotes.

FOLKLORE. The term used to describe tradition, customs, and stories passed from generation to generation. Embraces legends, proverbs and folktales.

FORM. The term used in reference to the style or design of an article as distinct from its content.

GALLEYS. The first typeset version of a manuscript, not yet bound into magazine or book form. The editor will often send galleys to the writer prior to publication so that any discrepancies may be corrected.

GHOSTWRITER. A writer who puts into literary form an article, speech or book based on another person's life, ideas, or knowledge. A ghostwriter usually doesn't have his name on the piece unless it is "as told to". Many biographies of famous people, or accounts of events, are written by ghostwriters.

GLOSSY. A black and white photograph (print) with a shiny surface as opposed to a matt finish.

HARD COPY. The printed copy of a manuscript, usually in reference to the computer print-out.

HARDWARE. All the components of a computer that are not software (programmes and disk). The parts that are actually the computer. ie: transistors and circuit boards.

HOMONYM. A word that is identical in form with another word, in sound or spelling, or both. ie: be, bee; bear, bare; too, to, two.

HONORARIUM. Token payment in recognition of work done. This can be a small amount of money, contributor's copies of the publication, or a byline.

HYPERBOLE. An exaggeration of a word or phrase for emphasis. ie: I walked a million miles.

IDIOM. A word or phrase that cannot be translated literally from one language to another. ie: flat broke.

ILLUSTRATIONS. Art work that accompanies a submission. May be photographs, drawings, or paintings. They are usually paid for separately from the manuscript.

INVASION OF PRIVACY. Writing about person, even truthfully, without their consent.

KILL FEE. A percentage, of the contracted price, that is paid if the editor rejects a completed, submitted article.

LEAD TIME. The time between the acquisition of an article by an editor and the actual publication date.

LETTER-QUALITY. High quality computer print-out that looks like it's typewritten.

LIBEL. A published statement or photograph that damages another person, through contempt, ridicule, or accusation. The defense is: truth, fair comment, or privilege.

LITERAL. The simplest primary meaning of a word, statement or text. The most straightforward meaning. A literal translation is one that tried to transfer the exact meaning of a text from one language to another.

LITTLE. Refers to small, literary publications with a limited circulation.

LOCAL COLOUR. Writing that is devoted to capturing the customs, speech and folklore of another society or regional community.

MEDIUM. The technical process employed in an art. In literature, the medium is language.

METAPHOR. The most important figure of speech in which one idea or action is referred to by a word or phrase normally indicating another idea or action. The resemblance is assumed as an imaginary identity rather than a directly stated comparison. ie: That man is a rat, is a metaphor while that man is like a rat, is not.

Metaphors create new combinations of ideas. A MIXED METAPHOR, is a combination of actions or ideas that is illogical. Usually, the use of two metaphors applied to one thing. ie: this tower of strength will forge ahead.

MICROCOMPUTER. A small computer system capable of performing specific tasks with the data it receives. Personal computers are microcomputers.

MODEL RELEASE. A paper signed by the subject of a photograph, or the guardian if the subject is a minor, giving permission for the picture to be used.

MODEM: A small electrical component that plugs into a computer serial port and a telephone line. Modems are used to transmit data from one computer to another.

MONOGRAPH: A detailed and scholarly documented subject concerning a single subject.

MULTIPLE SUBMISSIONS: Sending more than one manuscript, or idea, to several publishers at the same time. Means the same thing as simultaneous submissions.

MUSE. A source of inspiration to a writer. The Muse is usually represented as a female deity, having its beginning with the nine daughters of Zeus (Greek Mythology).

NARRATION: A process of relating a sequence of events. Narration is written in the first sense, separate from dialogue, description or commentary.

NARRATIVE. The telling of an occurrence, true or fictitious, that recounts a sequence of events. Narrative includes telling of an action (the dog sat by the fire), short news items, travelogues, diaries, and historical or biographical works.

NET RECEIPTS. A payment to a writer based on the amount of money a publisher receives after booksellers' discounts, special sale discounts and returns. 15% of net can supply a writer with very little income.

NEW AGE. A term used to link works with the metaphysical, spiritual, and other forms of alternative living. The New Age theories embrace UFOs, spiritual healing, psychic phenomena, astrology...all things dealing with reality beyond everyday perception.

NEWSBREAK. A brief, late-breaking story added to a newspaper just before going to press. Also, a magazine news item of importance to the readers.

NLQ. Abbreviation for near letter-quality. Dot-matrix print, from a computer printout.

OFFPRINT. Copies of a writer's article taken "out of issue" before a magazine is bound for sale. Offprints are given to the author of the work in lieu of payment and can be used by the writer as a published writing sample when sending query letters or manuscript submissions.

ON SPEC. When an editor expresses interest in a query for an article, he agrees to read the finished manuscript, "on speculation". He is under no obligation to publish.

ONE-SHOT FEATURES. A single feature article for a syndicate to sell as compared with series or syndicated columns.

ONE-TIME RIGHTS. Granting licence to a publisher to use a writer's material for one time only.

ONOMATOPOEIA. The use of words that seem to imitate the sound they refer to. ie: murmur, whisper, babble,

hum, fizz, hiss. The use of these words adds "colour" to the material.

OUTLINE. A summary of the contents of a book, usually 5 to 20 pages when submitted to a publisher, that shows the scope of the article or book. When an outline is used by the writer, it is a guide to the sequence of events.

OVER-THE-TRANSOM. Unsolicited material submitted by a freelance writer.

OXYMORON. A figure of speech that combines two contradictory terms. ie: living death, bittersweet, loving hate, still-waking sleep.

PACKAGE SALE. The purchase of a manuscript and photographs by an editor for one set price and paid for by one cheque.

PAGE RATE. The payment for an article per published page as opposed to per word. This is a popular form of payment by literary magazines. Usually, the print is small, with many words per page, so the writer gets a token of what he would if payment was per word.

PARADOX. A self-contradictory statement or expression that provokes the reader into seeking another meaning in which it would be true. ie: everything he says is a lie.

PARALLELISM. The arrangement of similarly constructed clauses and sentences. ie: I'd give my coloured coat for a sack-cloth cloak.

PARAPHRASE. A restatement of a passage's meaning, usually to clarify the original sense of the text.

PARODY. A mocking imitation of literary works or serious subjects. Satire.

PAYMENT ON ACCEPTANCE. The editor sends a cheque for a manuscript as soon as he reads it and decides to publish.

PAYMENT ON PUBLICATION. An editor doesn't send a cheque for a manuscript until it has been published. At times, this can be 30-90 days after publication.

PEN NAME. The use of other than the writer's legal name. The writer may wish to remain anonymous for any number of reasons or the editor may assign a pen name if the writer is doing a series they wish to present as the work of more than one author. Also, a pseudonym.

PERIODICAL. A magazine or newspaper published at regular intervals. ie: daily, weekly, monthly.

PHOTO FEATURE. Printed material whose focus is on the photographs rather than on the accompanying written word.

PHOTOCOPY. Copies of the original manuscript. Most editors accept photocopied submissions but a few feel that if copies are used, the submissions are simultaneous. State that this is not the case.

PIECE. A word synonymous with article. For example: "This piece is about the Great Wall of China."

PIRATED. A work published without the author's permission, therefore reducing his income. Copyright laws, enforced in the late 19th century, have reduced this practice.

PLAGIARISM. The theft of ideas or passages of written work, passed off as one's own, without acknowledgement to the original author. Literary theft.

POINT OF VIEW. Also, P.O.V. The vantage point from which a story seems to be viewed. ie: first person narrative, third person narrative. Some authors use multiple P.O.V. to show events from the position of two or more characters.

POLEMIC. A written attack on an opinion or policy, usually a political or theological criticism.

POTBOILER. Refers to the quick projects a writer does to bring in money on a regular basis (keeping the pot boiling) while working on major articles.

PRINTOUT. The copy printed from a computer. Also, hard copy.

PROOFREADING. Close reading of manuscript to pick up all spelling, punctuation and typographical errors.

PROSPECTUS. A written description, usually one page, of a proposed article or book.

PUBLIC DOMAIN. Material that was never copyrighted or whose copyright has expired.

PUBLICATION NOT COPYRIGHTED. Allowing your work to be published in an uncopyrighted magazine places it in the public domain and it cannot subsequently be copyrighted.

PUN. A word that achieves humour or emphasis by two distinct meanings. A word or phrase that has a second meaning. ie: Today's top news story is about trouble in the grain industry and we're going to grind away at it until we find the truth.

QUERY. A letter sent to an editor outlining a story idea. It is intended to raise enough interest so that the writer will get an assignment.

RELEASE. A signed statement that your idea is original, that it has never been sold to anyone else, and that you are selling the rights agreed upon by you and your editor.

REPORTING TIME. The time it takes for the editor to answer the author's query or submission.

REPRINT RIGHTS. Licensing an editor to reprint work that has appeared in another publication.

REVISION. The process of amending a version of a work, published or unpublished, often at the request of an editor.

RHETORIC. The exploitation of eloquence. Also, those aspects of a work that guide the responses of the reader.

RHETORICAL QUESTION. A question asked for the persuasive effect rather than for a genuine request of information. Usually, the answer is too obvious to require an answer.

ROUND OUT YOUR CHARACTERS. This is a favourite expression of editors. It can be used in fiction or in nonfiction profiles. It means that the people in your story are not showing enough personality or physical presence. You "round out" by adding words that tell what your character looks like, what he feels and how he thinks.

ROUND-UP ARTICLE. Comments from, or interviews with, a number of experts speaking on a single theme.

SASE. The abbreviation for self-addressed stamped envelope. One should be included in all correspondence and with every submission to editors.

SATIRE. Writing that exposes the failings of individuals or societies to ridicule.

SCANNING. A process by which printed text can be read by a computer and converted to workable data.

SEMANTICS. The study of meaning in language. The expression, it's a matter of semantics, is used when an argument arises about the meaning of a word of phrase. Often referred to as, "splitting hairs".

SEME. A basic description of a person. ie: white male, medium height and build, and greying at the temples.

SEMIMONTHLY. Twice a month.

SEMIWEEKLY. Twice a week.

SERIAL. A published periodical. A newspaper or magazine.

SIDEBAR. A companion piece to a news report or a magazine article. Often lists statistical information.

SIMILE. A comparison between two different things, actions, or feelings. Uses the words like or as. ie: He was so thin he was just like a bean pole.

SIMULTANEOUS SUBMISSIONS. Submitting the same material to more than one publisher at the same time.

SLANT. The style of an article that will appeal to readers of a certain magazine. For example, stories that always use a happy ending.

SLIDES. Usually called transparencies by editors requesting coloured photographs.

SLUSH PILE. The unsolicited manuscripts received by an editor.

SOFTWARE. Programmes and disks used in the computer system.

SPECULATION. Submitting a manuscript that the editor has agreed to look at, with no promise of publication.

STYLE. The way in which something is written. ie: Long, flowing prose, or short, clipped news items.

SYNONYM. A word that has the same meaning as another word and can be substituted in context. ie event/ happening.

SYNOPSIS. A summary of a plot or argument.

TABLOID. Newspaper publication whose format is about half the size of a regular paper.

TAGLINE. A caption for a photo or a comment added to a filler.

TEARSHEET. A page from a magazine or newspaper that contains your work.

TEXT. The actual wording of a written work.

UNSOLICITED MANUSCRIPT. Work sent to a publishing house that the editor did not specifically request.

USER FRIENDLY. Easy to handle or use. Refers to computers designed to make them easy to understand.